SQL Server
Interview Questions And Answers

X.Y. Wang

Contents

Chapter 1

Introduction

The ability to manage, analyze, and utilize data has become a critical skill in today's data-driven world. As businesses continue to embrace digital transformation, understanding the intricacies of database management systems such as SQL Server is essential for professionals working in data-related roles. With this book, "SQL Server Interview Questions and Answers," our aim is to provide an invaluable resource for anyone seeking to deepen their knowledge of SQL Server or prepare for job interviews in the field.

This book covers a comprehensive range of SQL Server topics, from basic concepts and queries to advanced techniques and best practices for optimizing performance, ensuring high availability, and implementing security measures. Each section is designed to cater to varying levels of expertise, enabling readers to quickly identify and focus on the topics most relevant to their needs.

Chapter 2 begins with basic SQL Server concepts and components, introducing readers to the fundamentals of relational database management systems, primary and foreign key constraints, and the use of tables in SQL Server. As the chapter progresses, readers will learn about data types, SELECT statements, and different types of JOIN operations.

In Chapter 3, the focus shifts to intermediate topics, including clustered and non-clustered indexes, backups, triggers, and isolation levels. Additionally, readers will explore ACID properties, deadlocks, subqueries, and performance optimization techniques for SQL Server queries.

Chapter 4 delves into advanced topics, covering areas such as star and snowflake schemas in data warehousing, dynamic management views and functions, SQL Server Analysis Services, and database mirroring. Readers will also learn about FileStream feature, Extended Events, partitioning, and best practices for index maintenance.

Chapter 5, the Expert section, covers topics such as lock escalation, SQL Server failover cluster instances, buffer pool extension, and Service Broker. This chapter will also discuss capacity planning, indexed views, disaster recovery strategies, and SQL Server Data Quality Services.

Finally, Chapter 6, the Guru section, addresses complex subjects such as scalable SQL Server architecture, advanced query optimization, multi-tenant environments, machine learning integration, and cross-platform database management. This chapter will also cover SQL Server auditing, data archiving, and real-time analytics solutions, among other advanced topics.

Whether you are a novice looking to build a foundation in SQL Server, a seasoned professional seeking to expand your knowledge, or a job candidate preparing for an interview, "SQL Server Interview Questions and Answers" offers an expert-level guide to help you navigate the ever-evolving world of data management. Happy learning!

Chapter 2

Basic

2.1 What is SQL Server, and what are its primary components?

SQL Server is a relational database management system (RDBMS) developed by Microsoft. It is used to store, manage, and retrieve data as requested by other software applications. SQL Server provides a robust and scalable platform for developing, deploying, and managing enterprise-level applications.

The primary components of SQL Server are:

1. Database Engine: This is the core component of SQL Server that stores, manages, and processes data. It provides capabilities for data storage, indexing, querying, and transaction processing.

2. Integration Services: This component provides tools and services for extract, transform, and load (ETL) operations. It helps to integrate data from different sources and transform them into a format that can be used by the Database Engine.

3. Analysis Services: This component provides tools and services for online analytical processing (OLAP) and data mining. It helps to analyze data and create multi-dimensional views of data for better

decision making.

4. Reporting Services: This component provides tools and services for creating, managing, and delivering reports. It helps to create and distribute reports based on the data stored in SQL Server.

5. Machine Learning Services: This component provides tools and services for running R and Python scripts inside the database. It helps to perform advanced analytics and machine learning tasks directly inside the SQL Server.

Each of these components offers a unique set of capabilities that can be used to build enterprise-level applications. They work together to provide a comprehensive solution for data storage, management, and analysis.

2.2   Can you explain the difference between SQL and T-SQL?

SQL (Structured Query Language) is a standard language used to communicate with relational database systems. SQL is used to create, read, update, and delete (CRUD) data in these databases. Various database vendors like Oracle, Microsoft, and MySQL support SQL language.

T-SQL (Transact-SQL) is a proprietary procedural language used by Microsoft SQL Server. T-SQL is an extension of SQL and provides additional programming constructs that are not available in standard SQL. T-SQL supports programming constructs like stored procedures, triggers, user-defined functions, and transactions.

Here are some of the differences between SQL and T-SQL:

1. Programming constructs: T-SQL supports procedural constructs like cursors, control statements, and exception handling, which are not supported in standard SQL. T-SQL also supports stored procedures, user-defined functions, and triggers.

2. Functionality: T-SQL provides additional functionality over SQL. For example, T-SQL includes the ability to handle errors, control

program flow using loops, and conditionals, manipulate data using cursors, and work with variables.

3. Syntax differences: While T-SQL syntax is based on SQL, it contains additional statements and keywords. For example, T-SQL includes the "BEGIN" and "END" keywords to define blocks of code.

4. Database support: SQL is a standard language and can be used with various relational database systems. T-SQL, on the other hand, is mostly used with Microsoft SQL Server.

Here is a simple example of the T-SQL code for creating a stored procedure:

```
CREATE PROCEDURE GetCustomer
@CustomerId INT
AS
BEGIN
SELECT * FROM Customers WHERE CustomerId = @CustomerId
END
```

This code creates a stored procedure named "GetCustomer" that accepts a parameter "CustomerId". The procedure selects data from the "Customers" table where "CustomerId" matches the input parameter.

In summary, SQL is a standard language used with relational database systems, while T-SQL is a proprietary language used with Microsoft SQL Server. T-SQL includes additional programming constructs and functionality not found in SQL.

2.3   What are the different editions of SQL Server?

SQL Server is a relational database management system (RDBMS) that supports the storing, manipulation, and retrieval of data. There are several different editions of SQL Server available, each with its own set of features and capabilities.

1. **SQL Server Enterprise Edition:** SQL Server Enterprise Edition is the most comprehensive edition of SQL Server, offering the full range of enterprise-level features and functionalities. This edition is designed for large organizations and mission-critical applications

that require high performance, scalability, and security. This edition includes features such as advanced analytics, in-memory technology, and advanced security capabilities.

2. **SQL Server Standard Edition:** SQL Server Standard Edition is a more limited version of the Enterprise Edition, which is designed for mid-sized to large organizations that require more scalability and performance than the Express or Developer editions offer. This edition offers features such as basic analytics and advanced backup and recovery capabilities.

3. **SQL Server Express Edition:** SQL Server Express Edition is a free, entry-level version of SQL Server that is designed for small-scale applications and development purposes. It has a smaller footprint and fewer features than the Standard or Enterprise editions, but it is sufficient for basic database management tasks.

4. **SQL Server Developer Edition:** SQL Server Developer Edition is an edition of SQL Server intended for development and testing purposes. This edition offers all the features of the Enterprise Edition, but it is licensed for development purposes only and cannot be used in production environments.

5. **SQL Server Web Edition:** SQL Server Web Edition is a specialized edition of SQL Server that is designed for hosting web applications and web services. This edition is optimized for internet-facing workloads and offers features such as high availability, scalability, and security.

6. **SQL Server Business Intelligence Edition:** SQL Server Business Intelligence Edition is a specialized edition of SQL Server that includes capabilities that are specifically designed for business intelligence applications. This edition offers features like data warehousing, data mining, and advanced analytics.

In summary, the different editions of SQL Server offer various sets of features and functionalities to cater to different scenarios, workload types, and budgetary constraints, making it a highly versatile RDBMS solution.

2.4   What is a relational database management system (RDBMS)?

A relational database management system (RDBMS) is a software system that manages relational databases. In a relational database, data is stored in tables, where each table consists of rows and columns. A row represents a collection of related data, and a column represents a specific attribute or field of the data.

The RDBMS enables users to interact with the database by supporting various operations such as insertion, deletion, and modification of data, as well as running queries that retrieve data from the database. The RDBMS also enforces data integrity and consistency by enforcing constraints and relationships between tables.

Some popular examples of RDBMS include MySQL, Oracle, Microsoft SQL Server, and PostgreSQL. These systems use a common language called Structured Query Language (SQL) to manipulate data in the database.

In summary, an RDBMS is a software system that manages relational databases by supporting various data operations and enforcing data integrity and consistency.

2.5   Can you explain the difference between primary key and foreign key constraints?

A primary key is a constraint that uniquely identifies each row in a table. It is a column or set of columns that uniquely identifies each record in a table, and it must contain unique values. Primary keys ensure the integrity of the data in a table and are used as a reference by other tables that reference them. The primary key is always a unique index, and it can be used to enforce data integrity and ensure that each row is unique.

On the other hand, a foreign key is a constraint that is used to establish a relationship between two tables. It is a column or set of columns in one table that refers to a primary key in another table. A foreign key constraint ensures that the values in the column(s) of the referencing table must match the values in the referenced table. Foreign keys are used to enforce referential integrity, ensuring that data stays consistent across related tables.

Here's an example to illustrate the difference between primary key and foreign key constraints.

Let's say we have two tables, Customers and Orders. The Customers table has a primary key constraint on the CustomerID column, which means that every record in the Customers table has a unique value in the CustomerID column. The Orders table has a foreign key constraint on the CustomerID column, which means that the values in the CustomerID column of the Orders table must match the values in the CustomerID column of the Customers table.

```
CREATE TABLE Customers (
  CustomerID int PRIMARY KEY,
  FirstName varchar(50),
  LastName varchar(50),
  Email varchar(50)
)

CREATE TABLE Orders (
  OrderID int,
  OrderDate datetime,
  CustomerID int,
  FOREIGN KEY (CustomerID) REFERENCES Customers(CustomerID)
)
```

In this example, the primary key in the Customers table is the CustomerID column, and the foreign key in the Orders table is also the CustomerID column. This establishes a relationship between the two tables, where each order in the Orders table is associated with a customer in the Customers table.

Overall, primary key constraints are used to uniquely identify each row in a table, while foreign key constraints are used to establish relationships between tables by referencing the primary key of another table.

2.6   What is a table, and how is it used in SQL Server?

In SQL Server, a table is a fundamental database object that stores data in a structured format. It is used to organize and group related information in a way that makes it easy to access and manage. A table consists of columns, which define the properties of the data being stored, and rows, which contain the actual data values.

Tables in SQL Server are used to store a wide variety of data, such as customer information, product details, financial records, and more. They are created using a CREATE TABLE statement, which specifies the column names, data types, and any constraints or rules that must be followed when inserting or updating data.

For example, the following SQL code creates a simple table called 'Employees' with three columns: 'EmployeeID', 'FirstName', and 'LastName'.

```
CREATE TABLE Employees (
    EmployeeID INT PRIMARY KEY,
    FirstName NVARCHAR(50),
    LastName NVARCHAR(50)
);
```

Once a table has been created, data can be inserted into it using an INSERT statement. For example, the following SQL code inserts a new employee record into the 'Employees' table:

```
INSERT INTO Employees (EmployeeID, FirstName, LastName)
VALUES (1, 'John', 'Doe');
```

Data can also be retrieved from a table using a SELECT statement, which retrieves one or more columns from one or more rows in the table. For example, the following SQL code retrieves the first name and last name of all employees in the 'Employees' table:

```
SELECT FirstName, LastName
FROM Employees;
```

Tables can also be modified using ALTER TABLE statements to add or remove columns or constraints, and can be dropped using a DROP TABLE statement to delete the entire table and its data.

Overall, tables are an important and essential component of SQL Server databases, allowing data to be stored, organized, and manipulated in a structured and efficient manner.

2.7   What are the basic SQL Server data types?

SQL Server data types are used to specify the type of data that is stored in a column of a table. The basic SQL Server data types can be divided into the following categories:

1. Character strings: These data types are used to store textual data. They include:

- 'CHAR(n)': Fixed-length string with a length of n. For example, 'CHAR(10)' can store a string with up to 10 characters.

- 'VARCHAR(n)': Variable-length string with a maximum length of n. For example, 'VARCHAR(10)' can store strings of up to 10 characters long.

- 'TEXT': A string data type that can store up to 231-1 bytes of non-Unicode data.

2. Unicode Character strings: These data types are used to store Unicode-encoded textual data. They include:

- 'NCHAR(n)' : A fixed-length string, storing exactly n Unicode characters. For example, 'NCHAR(10)' can store 10 Unicode characters.

- 'NVARCHAR(n)' : A variable-length Unicode string with a maximum length of n. For example, 'NVARCHAR(10)' can store Unicode strings up to 10 characters long.

- 'NTEXT': Similar to TEXT data type but stores Unicode-encoded data instead.

3. Numeric data types: These data types are used to store numeric data with different levels of precision and range. They include:

- 'BIT': A bit data type that can store 0 or 1.

- 'TINYINT': A small integer data type that can store values from 0 to 255.

- 'SMALLINT': An integer data type that can store values from -32,768 to 32,767.

- 'INT': A standard integer data type that can store values from -231 to 231-1.

- 'BIGINT': A large integer data type that can store values from -263 to 263-1.

- 'FLOAT(p)': A float data type that can store floating-point numbers. p stands for the number of bits used to store the mantissa.

- 'DECIMAL(p,s)': A decimal data type that can store decimal numbers with a precision of p digits and a scale of s digits.

4. Date and time data types: These data types are used to store date and time information. They include:

- 'DATE': Stores only the date and has a range of January 1, 1 AD through December 31, 9999.

- 'TIME': Stores only the time information.

- 'DATETIME': Stores both date and time information. This data is accurate to a single minute and has a range of January 1, 1753, through December 31, 9999.

- 'DATETIME2': Similar to DATETIME, but with a greater precision, down to 100 nanoseconds.

- 'SMALLDATETIME': Accurate to the minute but has a smaller range than DATETIME. This data type has a range of January 1, 1900, through June 6, 2079.

These are the basic SQL Server data types. There are also other data types, such as cursor, cursor variable, table, and XML data types, which provide specific functionality for handling data in SQL Server.

2.8 Can you explain what a SELECT statement is and how it is used in SQL Server?

In SQL Server, the SELECT statement is used to retrieve data from tables in a database. The syntax of a basic SELECT statement is as follows:

```
SELECT column1, column2, ... FROM table_name;
```

Here, 'column1', 'column2', and so on are the names of the columns
in the table that you want to retrieve data from, and 'table_name' is
the name of the table. You can also select all columns from a table
by using the '*' wildcard character:

```
SELECT * FROM table_name;
```

You can also use the SELECT statement with various optional clauses
to filter and sort the data, as well as to perform calculations and
aggregate functions. Here are some examples of these clauses:

- WHERE: used to filter data based on a specified condition. For
example, the following statement retrieves all rows from the 'orders'
table where the 'status' column is equal to 'Pending':

```
SELECT * FROM orders WHERE status = 'Pending';
```

- ORDER BY: used to sort the data in ascending or descending order
based on one or more columns. For example, the following statement
retrieves all rows from the 'products' table sorted in descending order
by the 'price' column:

```
SELECT * FROM products ORDER BY price DESC;
```

- GROUP BY: used to group the data by one or more columns, and
perform aggregate functions on each group. For example, the following statement retrieves the total revenue for each category from the
'orders' and 'order_details' tables:

```
SELECT c.category_name, SUM(o.quantity * o.unit_price) AS total_revenue
FROM categories AS c
INNER JOIN products AS p ON c.category_id = p.category_id
INNER JOIN order_details AS o ON p.product_id = o.product_id
GROUP BY c.category_name;
```

In addition to these clauses, the SELECT statement can also be used
with various other options and functions to perform more complex
calculations and operations on the data.

2.9 What is the purpose of the WHERE clause in a SQL query?

The WHERE clause in a SQL query is used to filter data based on specific criteria. It follows the SELECT statement and is followed by the FROM statement, and its purpose is to specify which rows of data to retrieve from the specified table(s).

The syntax of a basic SQL query with a WHERE clause is as follows:

```
SELECT column1, column2, ...
FROM table_name
WHERE condition;
```

The condition specified in the WHERE clause can be any logical expression that evaluates to true or false. This condition can reference one or more columns in the table, as well as use various comparison and logical operators.

For example, the following query retrieves all rows from a table named "employees" where the "salary" column is greater than 50000:

```
SELECT *
FROM employees
WHERE salary > 50000;
```

The WHERE clause can also contain multiple conditions, which can be combined using logical operators such as AND and OR. For example, the following query retrieves all rows from the "employees" table where the "salary" is greater than 50000 AND the "department" is either 'Sales' or 'Marketing':

```
SELECT *
FROM employees
WHERE salary > 50000 AND department IN ('Sales', 'Marketing');
```

In addition to basic comparison and logical operators, the WHERE clause can also use a variety of functions and built-in operators to filter data based on specific criteria. For example, the following query retrieves all rows from a table named "orders" where the "order_date" is within the last 7 days:

```
SELECT *
FROM orders
WHERE order_date >= DATEADD(day, -7, GETDATE());
```

Overall, the WHERE clause is an essential part of SQL queries as it allows analysts and developers to select only the data they need from large tables, and to filter the data based on specific criteria that meet their business needs.

2.10   Can you explain the difference between INNER JOIN and OUTER JOIN?

INNER JOIN and OUTER JOIN are types of SQL Joins used to combine data from two or more tables. SQL joins allow data to be extracted from multiple tables based on how the tables are related to each other through one or more keys or columns.

Inner Join:

- An Inner Join returns only the matching rows from both tables based on a specified condition.

- The resulting table will only contain rows where the join condition is true in both tables.

- Inner Join is the most commonly used type of Join.

- The below SQL query is an example of Inner Join.

```
SELECT *
FROM table1
INNER JOIN table2
ON table1.column_name = table2.column_name;
```

Outer Join:

- Outer Join returns all the rows from one table and only the matching rows from the second table based on the specified condition.

- If the specified condition does not match any row in the second table, NULL values are used for that table.

- There are three types of Outer Join:
1. LEFT OUTER JOIN: returns all rows from the left table and matching rows from the right table. If no matching rows are found in the right table, NULL values are used.
2. RIGHT OUTER JOIN: returns all rows from the right table and matching rows from the left table. If no matching rows are found in the left table, NULL values are used.

3. FULL OUTER JOIN: returns all rows from both tables where there is a match. If no match is found for a table, NULL values are used.

- The below SQL query is an example of Left Outer Join.

```
SELECT *
FROM table1
LEFT OUTER JOIN table2
ON table1.column_name = table2.column_name;
```

Example:

Consider two tables: "Customers" and "Orders". Customers table has a column "CustomerId" while Orders table has a column "CustomerId" and "OrderId".

Customers Table:

```
| CustomerId | CustomerName | ContactName | Country |
|------------|--------------|-------------|---------|
| 1          | Alfreds      | Maria       | Germany |
| 2          | Bob's␣␣␣␣␣␣␣␣␣|␣Carlos␣␣␣␣␣␣|␣USA␣␣␣␣␣|
|␣3␣␣␣␣␣␣␣␣␣␣␣|␣Bruckner␣␣␣␣␣␣|␣Helena␣␣␣␣␣␣|␣Austria␣|
```

Orders Table:

```
| OrderId | Product | CustomerId |
|---------|---------|------------|
| 1       | Coke    | 2          |
| 2       | Pepsi   | 1          |
| 3       | Fanta   | 2          |
| 4       | Sprite  | 4          |
| 5       | 7UP     | 3          |
```

Inner Join:

```
SELECT Customers.CustomerName, Orders.Product
FROM Customers
INNER JOIN Orders
ON Customers.CustomerId = Orders.CustomerId;
```

Output:

```
| CustomerName | Product |
|--------------|---------|
| Alfreds      | Pepsi   |
| Bob's␣␣␣␣␣␣␣␣␣|␣Coke␣␣␣␣|
|␣Bob's        | Fanta   |
```

Left Outer Join:

```
SELECT Customers.CustomerName, Orders.Product
FROM Customers
LEFT OUTER JOIN Orders
ON Customers.CustomerId = Orders.CustomerId;
```

Output:

```
| CustomerName | Product |
|--------------|---------|
| Alfreds      | Pepsi |
| Bob's␣␣␣␣␣␣␣␣|␣Coke␣␣␣␣|
|␣Bob's        | Fanta |
| Bruckner     | NULL    |
```

Right Outer Join:

```
SELECT Customers.CustomerName, Orders.Product
FROM Customers
RIGHT OUTER JOIN Orders
ON Customers.CustomerId = Orders.CustomerId;
```

Output:

```
| CustomerName | Product |
|--------------|---------|
| Alfreds      | Pepsi |
| Bob's␣␣␣␣␣␣␣␣|␣Coke␣␣␣␣|
|␣Bob's        | Fanta |
| NULL         | Sprite |
| NULL         | 7UP     |
```

Full Outer Join:

```
SELECT Customers.CustomerName, Orders.Product
FROM Customers
FULL OUTER JOIN Orders
ON Customers.CustomerId = Orders.CustomerId;
```

Output:

```
| CustomerName | Product |
|--------------|---------|
| Alfreds      | Pepsi |
| Bob's␣␣␣␣␣␣␣␣|␣Coke␣␣␣␣|
|␣Bob's        | Fanta |
| Bruckner     | NULL    |
| NULL         | Sprite |
| NULL         | 7UP     |
```

2.11 What are aggregate functions in SQL Server, and can you provide a few examples?

Aggregate functions are SQL functions that return a single value based on multiple rows of a table. They can be used to perform calculations on entire sets of data rather than individual rows. SQL Server provides several built-in aggregate functions like COUNT, SUM, AVG, MAX, and MIN.

Here are some examples of these aggregate functions in action:

1. COUNT: This function counts the number of rows in a table based on a given condition.

```
SELECT COUNT(*) FROM orders;
```

This SQL statement returns the total number of orders.

2. SUM: This function returns the sum of a numerical column in a table.

```
SELECT SUM(price) FROM products WHERE category = 'electronics';
```

This SQL statement returns the total price of all electronic products.

3. AVG: This function returns the average value of a numerical column in a table.

```
SELECT AVG(age) FROM employees WHERE department = 'sales';
```

This SQL statement returns the average age of all employees in the sales department.

4. MAX: This function returns the maximum value of a column in a table.

```
SELECT MAX(salary) FROM employees WHERE title = 'manager';
```

This SQL statement returns the highest salary among all managers.

5. MIN: This function returns the minimum value of a column in a table.

```
SELECT MIN(quantity) FROM orders WHERE product_id = 123;
```

This SQL statement returns the smallest quantity of product with ID 123 that was ordered.

Aggregate functions can also be combined with other SQL statements like GROUP BY to group and summarize data by certain criteria. In conclusion, aggregate functions are powerful tools for summarizing large sets of data in SQL Server.

2.12   What is the purpose of the GROUP BY clause in a SQL query?

The GROUP BY clause is an essential part of SQL queries which allows the grouping of rows based on the values of one or more columns. The primary purpose of the GROUP BY clause is to aggregate data by applying various aggregate functions such as SUM, AVG, MAX, MIN, COUNT to the grouped rows.

The syntax of the GROUP BY clause is as follows:

```
SELECT column1, column2, aggregate_function(column3)
FROM table_name
GROUP BY column1, column2;
```

In this syntax, the SELECT statement lists the columns we want to retrieve, and the GROUP BY clause specifies the columns that we want to use for grouping the data. The aggregate function operates on the column, which is not included in the GROUP BY clause.

For example, let's consider a table "Orders" with the following columns: OrderID, CustomerID, OrderDate, OrderAmount. To find the total revenue generated by each customer, we can use the following query:

```
SELECT CustomerID, SUM(OrderAmount) AS TotalRevenue
FROM Orders
GROUP BY CustomerID;
```

This query uses the SUM() function to add up all the order amounts for each customer, and the GROUP BY clause groups the rows based on the CustomerID column.

Another example is finding the number of orders placed by each customer in a given time period. To do this, we can use the COUNT() function as follows:

```
SELECT CustomerID, COUNT(OrderID) AS TotalOrders
FROM Orders
WHERE OrderDate BETWEEN '2021-01-01' AND '2021-03-31'
GROUP BY CustomerID;
```

This query counts the number of orders placed by each customer between 1st Jan and 31st March 2021, and groups the rows based on the CustomerID column.

In summary, the GROUP BY clause is used to group rows based on one or more columns and apply aggregate functions to generate summary information for each group.

2.13   Can you describe the difference between UNION and UNION ALL?

In SQL Server, 'UNION' and 'UNION ALL' are used to combine data from two or more tables.

'UNION' returns only distinct rows from the combined tables, whereas 'UNION ALL' returns all rows, including duplicates, from the combined tables.

Here's an example to illustrate the difference between the two:

Let's say we have two tables, 'employees' and 'staff', with the following data:

```
employees table:
id   name   department
1    John   Sales
2    Jane   Marketing
3    Bob    IT

staff table:
id   name   department
1    John   Sales
3    Bob    IT
4    Sue    HR
```

If we execute the following 'UNION' query:

```
SELECT id, name, department FROM employees
UNION
SELECT id, name, department FROM staff
```

The result would be:

```
id   name   department
1    John   Sales
2    Jane   Marketing
3    Bob    IT
4    Sue    HR
```

Notice that only distinct rows are returned, so John and Bob are not duplicated.

If we execute the following 'UNION ALL' query:

```
SELECT id, name, department FROM employees
UNION ALL
SELECT id, name, department FROM staff
```

The result would be:

```
id   name   department
1    John   Sales
2    Jane   Marketing
3    Bob    IT
1    John   Sales
3    Bob    IT
4    Sue    HR
```

Notice that all rows are returned, including duplicates. In this case, John and Bob appear twice since they are in both tables.

In general, 'UNION' is useful when you want to eliminate duplicates from the combined results, while 'UNION ALL' is useful when you want to include duplicates. However, 'UNION' requires more processing to remove duplicates, so it can be slower than 'UNION ALL' for large datasets.

2.14   What are stored procedures, and why are they used in SQL Server?

A stored procedure in SQL Server is a block of precompiled SQL code that is stored in the database under a name or reference. It can be called multiple times by client applications or other database objects like triggers, functions or views. A stored procedure allows database administrators and developers to encapsulate a series of SQL statements into a single program unit, thereby enhancing the security, maintainability, and performance of the database application.

Stored procedures can be used to perform a variety of tasks, including data manipulation (SELECT, INSERT, UPDATE and DELETE operations), data administration (creation, modification, or deletion of database objects like tables, indexes, views, triggers or stored procedures), data validation (ensuring that data conforms to specific constraints such as non-null values or unique keys) and business logic (performing computations or other operations to support business requirements).

Stored procedures have a number of benefits over direct SQL statements:

1. Security: Stored procedures allow the database administrator to restrict direct access to the underlying tables, thereby preventing unauthorized access or modification of sensitive data. By granting execute permissions only to stored procedures, administrators can provide appropriate levels of access to users, depending on their roles.

2. Reusability: Stored procedures can be reused over time, resulting in performance benefits. Once compiled, a stored procedure can be called by multiple client applications, reducing the overhead of parsing, optimizing and generating the execution plan for duplicate SQL statements.

3. Maintenance: Stored procedures provide a centralized location for database logic, making it easier to maintain and modify the database application over time. Changes to a stored procedure can be made without modifying client applications.

4. Performance: Stored procedures can be optimized in the database to improve performance. SQL Server compiles and optimizes stored procedures once, and the optimized code can be cached in memory for reuse, resulting in faster response times for subsequent executions.

Here is an example of how to create a simple stored procedure in SQL Server:

```
CREATE PROCEDURE dbo.GetCustomers
AS
```

```
BEGIN
  SELECT FirstName, LastName, Email
  FROM Customers
END;
```

This stored procedure retrieves the first name, last name, and email address of all customers from the 'Customers' table. Once the stored procedure is created, it can be executed by calling 'dbo.GetCustomers' from a client application or other database object.

2.15   What are views in SQL Server, and what are their benefits?

In SQL Server, a view is a virtual table that is based on the result set of an SQL statement. Views can be used to simplify complex queries or to restrict access to certain data by providing a filtered, customized view of the data in a specific table or set of tables.

Benefits of using views in SQL Server include:

1. Security: Views can be used to restrict access to sensitive data by providing a filtered view of the data that only includes the columns and rows that the user is authorized to access.

2. Simplify complex queries: Views can be used to simplify complex queries by providing a predefined set of joins or filters, which can be reused across multiple queries.

3. Performance: Views can be used to improve query performance by precomputing complex calculations or aggregations and storing them in a separate view. This can significantly reduce the time required to execute the query.

4. Abstraction: Views can be used to provide an abstraction layer over the underlying data structures, which can make it easier to modify the underlying data schema without affecting the queries that rely on it.

Here is an example of creating a simple view:

```
CREATE VIEW [dbo].[myView] AS
SELECT [Column1], [Column2]
```

```
FROM [myTable]
WHERE [Column3] = 'myValue'
```

This will create a view named "myView" that only includes columns "Column1" and "Column2" from the "myTable" table, where "Column3" is equal to "myValue".

To use the view, you can simply query it as if it were a table:

```
SELECT *
FROM [myView]
```

This will return the filtered result set from "myTable" based on the view definition.

2.16 What is normalization in the context of a relational database, and why is it important?

Normalization is the process of organizing data in a relational database in such a way that reduces redundancy and dependency. It involves breaking down a large table into smaller tables and defining relationships between them. Normalization ensures that each piece of data is stored only once, thereby reducing data duplication and improving data consistency.

Normalization is important because it helps to eliminate data inconsistencies that can occur due to data redundancy, and improves data integrity by increasing data consistency. Another key benefit of normalization is it reduces the storage space required for storing the data, as well as the amount of time and effort required to maintain the database.

In relational database design, normalization is typically achieved using a set of rules called normal forms. There are several normal forms, including first normal form (1NF), second normal form (2NF), third normal form (3NF), and so on, each with its own set of rules and guidelines.

For example, let's consider a table that stores information about student grades, courses, and instructors:

```
StudentGrades
-------------
CourseID
InstructorID
StudentID
Grade
```

This table is not fully normalized because of data redundancy. For instance, if the same course is taught by multiple instructors, the CourseID will be repeated in several rows.

To fix this redundancy, we can break down the table into three smaller tables:

```
Courses
-------
CourseID
CourseName

Instructors
-----------
InstructorID
InstructorName

StudentCourseGrades
-------------------
CourseID
InstructorID
StudentID
Grade
```

By normalizing the data in this way, the CourseID and InstructorID are stored only once, improving data consistency and reducing data duplication, which has many implications in the database such as decreasing the risk of data anomalies and making the database more efficient.

In conclusion, normalization is essential because it can help eliminate data inconsistencies, improve data integrity, and enhance overall database performance.

2.17   What is an index in SQL Server, and what is its purpose?

In SQL Server, an index is a database object that improves the performance of queries executed on a table. It is created on one or more columns of a table, and stores a sorted copy of the data in those columns. This sorted copy makes it faster for the SQL Server to locate specific values within those columns when executing a query.

An index is similar to the index found at the back of a book. The index contains an ordered list of the pages in the book where a particular word or phrase can be found. Similarly, an index on a table in SQL Server contains an ordered list of the rows in the table, along with a pointer to the location of each row on the disk.

When a query is executed that involves a column or columns covered by an index, SQL Server can use the index to locate the relevant rows much faster than if it had to scan the entire table. This can result in significant performance improvements, especially for large tables.

There are different types of indexes that can be created in SQL Server, depending on the needs of the database and the queries that will be executed. The most common types are:

```
- Clustered index: This is an index that determines the physical order of the
      data on disk. A table can have only one clustered index, and it is
      typically created on the primary key column of the table.
- Non-clustered index: This is an index that does not affect the physical
      order of the data on disk. A table can have multiple non-clustered
      indexes, and they are typically created on columns frequently used in
      search conditions, join conditions, or order by clauses.
```

Creating an index requires some overhead, as SQL Server has to maintain the sorted copy of the data and update it whenever the underlying data changes. Therefore, it is important to carefully consider which columns to index and how many indexes to create, in order to achieve the best query performance while minimizing the overhead of index maintenance.

Here is an example of creating a non-clustered index on a table in SQL Server:

```
CREATE NONCLUSTERED INDEX idx_customer_lastname
ON Customer (LastName);
```

This creates a non-clustered index named "idx_customer_lastname" on the "LastName" column of the "Customer" table. The index will store the sorted copy of the LastName column, along with a pointer to the corresponding row in the table. Queries that involve searching or ordering by LastName are likely to benefit from this index.

2.18   Can you explain the concept of trans- actions in SQL Server?

Transactions are a fundamental concept in database management systems, including SQL Server. A transaction is a logical unit of work
that either succeeds or fails completely as a whole. It provides a
way to group one or more SQL statements into a single unit of work
that is either performed in its entirety or not at all, ensuring data
consistency and integrity.

In SQL Server, transactions are initiated with the BEGIN TRANS-
ACTION statement and ended with either the COMMIT or ROLL-
BACK statement. During a transaction, SQL Server tracks all changes
made to the database and keeps a record known as a transaction log.
If the transaction is committed, the changes are permanently saved
to the database. If the transaction is rolled back, the changes are
undone and the database is restored to its previous state before the
transaction was initiated.

Consider the following example:

```
BEGIN TRANSACTION
UPDATE Orders
SET Quantity = Quantity + 5
WHERE CustomerID = 12345
COMMIT
```

In this example, a transaction is initiated and an update statement
is executed. The update statement adds 5 to the quantity of all
orders for a specific customer. If the transaction is committed, the
changes will be saved to the database. However, if an error occurs, or
if the transaction is rolled back, the changes will be undone and the
database will be restored to its previous state.

Transactions are essential in handling multiple users accessing the
same database simultaneously. Without transactions, multiple users
updating the same data simultaneously can lead to data inconsistency
and integrity issues.

In addition to the basic transaction structure, SQL Server also supports distributed transactions, savepoints, and nested transactions,
adding to the flexibility and functionality of transactions in database
management systems.

2.19   What is the difference between DELETE and TRUNCATE statements?

In SQL Server, both DELETE and TRUNCATE statements are used to remove data from a table, but they work in different ways and have different effects on the table and the surrounding environment.

DELETE statement is a Data Manipulation Language (DML) command which removes one or more rows from a table based on certain criteria. It is a very flexible statement that allows you to remove specific rows using WHERE clause, or to remove all rows from a table by omitting the WHERE clause.

The syntax of the DELETE statement is as follows:

```
DELETE FROM table_name
WHERE condition;
```

For example, suppose you have a table 'Customers' with the following data:

```
| Id | Name    | Age |
|----|---------|-----|
| 1  | Alice   | 25  |
| 2  | Bob     | 30  |
| 3  | Charlie | 35  |
```

If you want to delete the row of 'Bob' from this table, you can use the following DELETE statement:

```
DELETE FROM Customers
WHERE Name = 'Bob';
```

After executing this statement, the table 'Customers' will have the following data:

```
| Id | Name    | Age |
|----|---------|-----|
| 1  | Alice   | 25  |
| 3  | Charlie | 35  |
```

Note that the 'DELETE' statement only removes the rows that match the specified condition, and leaves the rest of the table intact.

On the other hand, TRUNCATE statement is a Data Definition Language (DDL) command which removes all the rows from a table, also known as "truncate the table". It is much faster than DELETE, because it doesn't remove the rows one-by-one, but instead deallocates the data pages of the table, effectively resetting the table to its initial state.

The syntax of the TRUNCATE statement is as follows:

```
TRUNCATE TABLE table_name;
```

For example, executing the following TRUNCATE statement on the 'Customers' table:

```
TRUNCATE TABLE Customers;
```

will remove all the rows from the table, and leave an empty table with the same structure.

Note that TRUNCATE statement doesn't support the use of WHERE clause, and it cannot be rolled back once executed. Also, since it resets the table to its initial state, it also resets the identity (auto-increment) value of the table, if it has one.

In summary, DELETE is used to remove specific rows based on a criteria, while TRUNCATE is used to remove all rows from a table, effectively resetting the table to its initial state. The choice between them depends on the specific use case, and whether you need to preserve some of the data or not.

2.20   What is the purpose of the SQL Server Management Studio (SSMS)?

SQL Server Management Studio (SSMS) is a tool provided by Microsoft for managing and administering SQL Server instances. It provides a centralized interface for accessing and configuring SQL Server components and features.

Here are some specific purposes of SSMS:

1. Database management: SSMS allows for the creation, modification, and deletion of databases and database objects such as tables,

views, stored procedures, and triggers.

2. Query execution: SSMS provides a query editor where SQL statements can be written, executed, and debugged. It also has options for displaying query results in various formats and can be used with the SQL Server Profiler to analyze query performance and troubleshoot issues.

3. Security management: SSMS includes tools for managing SQL Server security such as logins, users, roles, and permissions.

4. Maintenance planning: SSMS has a Maintenance Plan Wizard that simplifies the creation and execution of scheduled maintenance tasks such as backups, defragmentation, and index maintenance.

5. Monitoring: SSMS provides real-time monitoring of SQL Server performance and activity through different tools such as Activity Monitor and SQL Server Management Data Warehouse.

SSMS is a powerful tool that can help SQL Server database experts streamline and automate their tasks. It is an essential tool for SQL Server professionals and can improve their productivity and efficiency.

Here's an example of creating a table using SSMS:

1. Open SSMS and connect to a SQL Server instance.

2. Expand the Databases folder and right-click on the database where you want to create the table.

3. Select New Query to open the query editor.

4. Type the following SQL statement to create a table named "Employees":

```
CREATE TABLE Employees (
    EmployeeID INT PRIMARY KEY,
    FirstName VARCHAR(50),
    LastName VARCHAR(50),
    BirthDate DATE,
    HireDate DATE
);
```

5. Execute the SQL statement by clicking Execute or pressing F5.

6. The Employees table is now created and can be seen under the Tables folder in the Object Explorer.

Chapter 3

Intermediate

3.1 Can you explain the difference between a clustered and non-clustered index in SQL Server?

In SQL Server, an index is a database structure that is used to improve the performance of queries by allowing faster access to data. There are two main types of indexes, clustered and non-clustered.

A clustered index determines the physical order of data in a table. It is created on a single column or a group of columns called a key. When a table has a clustered index, the data is ordered by the key values and physically stored in the same order on disk. There can be only one clustered index per table.

A non-clustered index is a separate structure from the data and is used to improve the performance of queries by allowing faster access to data. It is also created on one or more columns called key columns. A non-clustered index contains a copy of the data in the indexed columns and a pointer to the location of the full data row in the table. There can be multiple non-clustered indexes per table.

The main difference between a clustered and non-clustered index is

the order of the data. In a clustered index, the physical order of the
data on disk matches the order of the key columns in the index. In
a non-clustered index, the physical order of the data on disk is not
related to the order of the key columns in the index.

Another difference between the two types of indexes is the impact
on performance. A clustered index can greatly improve the performance of queries that involve range searches or sorting based on the
key column(s) in the index. Since the data is physically ordered on
disk, SQL Server can retrieve the rows more efficiently. However,
a clustered index can also slow down insert and update operations,
since SQL Server needs to rearrange the data to maintain the physical
order of the index.

On the other hand, a non-clustered index can improve the performance of queries that filter data based on the indexed columns, but
it may not be as efficient for range searches or sorting. Non-clustered
indexes can also speed up data modification operations, since they
don't require any rearrangement of the data.

Here is an example of creating a clustered index on the "ID" column
of a table:

```
CREATE CLUSTERED INDEX IX_MyTable_ID ON dbo.MyTable (ID);
```

And here is an example of creating a non-clustered index on the "Last-
Name" and "FirstName" columns of a table:

```
CREATE NONCLUSTERED INDEX IX_MyTable_Name
ON dbo.MyTable (LastName, FirstName);
```

In summary, a clustered index determines the physical order of data
in a table based on its key column(s), while a non-clustered index
is a separate structure that contains a copy of the indexed columns
and a pointer to the location of the full data row in the table. The
choice of index type depends on the specific query patterns and data
modification requirements of your application.

3.2 What are the different types of back-ups in SQL Server, and when should you use each type?

There are several types of backups available in SQL Server, each with its own specific purpose and benefits. The following are the most commonly used types of backups:

1. Full Backup: A full backup is a complete backup of the entire database, including all data pages and log information. It is the baseline backup for the database, and it's used to restore the database to its original state. Full backups are typically performed regularly, such as daily or weekly, depending on the application's requirements. A full backup can be used to restore the database to any point in time.

Example:

```
BACKUP DATABASE MyDatabase
TO DISK = 'C:MyBackupMyDatabase.bak'
WITH FORMAT, NAME = 'Full Backup';
```

2. Differential Backup: Differential backups only backup the data that has changed since the last full backup. This type of backup is useful for databases that are very large and require frequent backups, as it reduces the backup time and storage space required. Differential backups can be used to restore the database to any point in time between the current differential backup and the last full backup.

Example:

```
BACKUP DATABASE MyDatabase
TO DISK = 'C:MyBackupMyDatabaseDiff.bak'
WITH DIFFERENTIAL, NAME = 'Differential Backup';
```

3. Transaction Log Backup: Transaction log backups capture all changes made to the database since the last transaction log backup. This type of backup is important for recovery purposes, as it allows you to restore the database to a specific point in time. Transaction log backups can be performed frequently, such as every 15 minutes or 30 minutes, depending on the application's requirements.

Example:

```
BACKUP LOG MyDatabase
TO DISK = 'C:MyBackupMyDatabaseLog.trn'
WITH NAME = 'Transaction Log Backup';
```

4. Copy-only Backup: Copy-only backups are used to create an ad-hoc backup that does not interrupt the backup sequence. This type of backup is useful when you want to create a one-time backup without affecting the regularly scheduled backups. Copy-only backups can be either a full backup or a differential backup.

Example:

```
BACKUP DATABASE MyDatabase
TO DISK = 'C:MyBackupMyDatabaseCopy.bak'
WITH COPY_ONLY, NAME = 'Copy-Only Backup';
```

5. File or Filegroup Backup: File or filegroup backups allow you to backup specific files or filegroups within a database. This type of backup is useful for databases where not all files are equally important or where specific files need to be restored. File or filegroup backups can be restored independently or in combination with other file or filegroup backups.

Example:

```
BACKUP DATABASE MyDatabase
FILEGROUP = 'PRIMARY'
TO DISK = 'C:MyBackupMyDatabaseFilegroup.bak'
WITH NAME = 'Filegroup Backup';
```

In summary, the type of backup to use depends on the database's requirements and the recovery plan. It is recommended to have a combination of full, differential, and transaction log backups to ensure data recovery in case of a disaster.

3.3   What is a SQL Server trigger, and what are the different types of triggers?

In SQL Server, a trigger is a special type of stored procedure that is automatically executed in response to certain events or actions performed on a database table or view. A trigger typically consists of a set of SQL statements that are executed when a specific event occurs.

There are two main types of triggers in SQL Server:

1. DML Triggers: These triggers are fired in response to DML (data manipulation language) events such as INSERT, UPDATE, and DELETE statements executed on a table or view. DML triggers can be further classified into two subtypes:

* 'After triggers': These triggers are executed after the DML event occurs, and they can be used to validate, modify, or log the changes made to the table.

For example, suppose we have a table called 'Orders' with columns 'OrderID', 'CustomerID', 'OrderDate', and 'Amount'. We can create an After trigger that automatically updates the 'Amount' column whenever an 'INSERT' or 'UPDATE' statement is executed on the 'Orders' table, as shown below:

```
CREATE TRIGGER UpdateAmount
ON Orders
AFTER INSERT, UPDATE
AS
BEGIN
  UPDATE Orders
  SET Amount = Quantity * UnitPrice
  FROM inserted
  WHERE Orders.OrderID = inserted.OrderID
END
```

* 'Instead of triggers': These triggers are executed instead of the actual DML event. They are commonly used to implement complex business logic, such as enforcing complex security policies, view restrictions, or other restrictions on certain tables.

For example, suppose we have a table called 'Employees' with columns 'EmployeeID', 'FirstName', 'LastName', and 'Salary'. We can create an Instead of trigger that prevents any 'DELETE' statements from being executed on the 'Employees' table for employees whose 'Salary' is greater than a certain threshold, as shown below:

```
CREATE TRIGGER PreventDelete
ON Employees
INSTEAD OF DELETE
AS
BEGIN
  DELETE Employees
  FROM Employees INNER JOIN deleted
  ON Employees.EmployeeID = deleted.EmployeeID
```

```
    WHERE Salary > 50000
END
```

2. DDL Triggers: These triggers are fired in response to DDL (data
definition language) events such as 'CREATE', 'ALTER', and 'DROP'
statements executed on a database or server. DDL triggers are mainly
used to enforce certain policies or to audit changes made to the
database schema.

For example, suppose we have a database called 'SalesDB' with several tables and views. We can create a DDL trigger that logs any
changes made to the database schema, as shown below:

```
CREATE TRIGGER LogSchemaChanges
ON DATABASE
FOR DDL_DATABASE_LEVEL_EVENTS
AS
BEGIN
    DECLARE @EventData XML
    SET @EventData = EVENTDATA()

    INSERT INTO SchemaChangesLog (EventDate, UserName, ObjectType,
        ObjectName, TSQLCommand)
    VALUES (GETDATE(), ORIGINAL_LOGIN(), @EventData.value('(/EVENT_INSTANCE
        /ObjectType)[1]', 'nvarchar(255)'),
    @EventData.value('(/EVENT_INSTANCE/ObjectName)[1]', 'nvarchar(255)'),
        @EventData.value('(/EVENT_INSTANCE/TSQLCommand)[1]', 'nvarchar(
        max)'))
END
```

In summary, SQL Server triggers are a powerful feature that can
be used to implement complex business logic, perform auditing, or
enforce various policies on database tables and views. The different
types of triggers provide a rich set of functionality to handle different
database events and to address different use cases.

3.4   Can you explain the concept of isola-
tion levels in SQL Server and provide
examples?

Isolation levels in SQL Server determine the level of interaction between transactions accessing shared resources such as tables, rows, or
pages. The isolation level ensures that one transaction does not interfere with another transaction while accessing the shared resource.
There are four isolation levels supported by SQL Server:

1. Read Uncommitted: This is the lowest isolation level and also called a dirty read. In this level, the transactions can read uncommitted changes made by other transactions in the same database. This means that the transactions are not isolated from each other and can lead to inconsistent or incorrect results.

2. Read Committed: This level allows transactions to read only the changes committed by other transactions. This means that the transactions are isolated from each other, but it may not prevent the phenomena such as non-repeatable reads and phantom rows.

3. Repeatable Read: This level ensures that a transaction sees the same data throughout the transaction. The data read by the transaction is locked and other transactions cannot modify it until the current transaction completes.

4. Serializable: This level provides the highest isolation level and ensures that transactions are completely isolated from one another. In this level, the transactions are processed sequentially, ensuring that no transaction modifies data that another transaction is currently modifying. This guarantees that the data is always consistent.

Here is an example to demonstrate the impact of different isolation levels in SQL Server. Let's assume that we have a table named "Order" with columns "OrderID", "CustomerName", and "Product". Suppose two transactions are accessing this table to read and update the data simultaneously.

Transaction 1:

```
SET TRANSACTION ISOLATION LEVEL READ COMMITTED;
BEGIN TRANSACTION
SELECT * FROM Order WHERE Product = 'Laptop'
UPDATE Order SET Product = 'Desktop' WHERE CustomerName = 'John'
COMMIT TRANSACTION
```

Transaction 2:

```
SET TRANSACTION ISOLATION LEVEL READ UNCOMMITTED;
BEGIN TRANSACTION
SELECT * FROM Order WHERE Product = 'Laptop'
COMMIT TRANSACTION
```

In this example, transaction 1 is set to READ COMMITTED level of isolation, and transaction 2 is set to READ UNCOMMITTED level of isolation.

In this case, transaction 1 will first select all the orders with a product name of "Laptop", update the product name to "Desktop" for all the orders with customer name "John", and then commit the transaction. During this time, transaction 2 can see the uncommitted changes that are made by transaction 1 because the READ UNCOMMITTED level allows the dirty read.

In contrast, if transaction 2 is set to REPEATABLE READ or SERIALIZABLE level of isolation, the transaction will not see any uncommitted changes made by transaction 1 because these levels of isolation provide better consistency and higher levels of data integrity.

In summary, the correct selection of isolation levels depends on the specific requirements of the application and the data consistency requirements. It is important to understand the trade-offs between data consistency and concurrency, and select an appropriate level of isolation based on the application's needs.

3.5 What are the ACID properties in database transactions, and why are they important?

The ACID properties are a set of characteristics that ensure database transactions are processed reliably in a consistent and predictable manner. ACID stands for Atomicity, Consistency, Isolation, and Durability.

- Atomicity: Atomicity refers to the all-or-nothing properties of transactions. It means that a transaction is treated as a single, indivisible unit of work, where either all the changes in the transaction are committed or none of the changes are committed. In SQL Server, a transaction can be accomplished using the BEGIN TRANSACTION, COMMIT TRANSACTION, and ROLLBACK TRANSACTION statements. For example, suppose we want to transfer funds between two bank accounts. This transaction involves debiting one account and crediting another account once. If either of the operations fails, it means that the transaction should fail entirely for data consistency. Therefore, to ensure atomicity, we enclose both operations within one transaction.

- Consistency: Consistency ensures that transactions bring the database from one valid state to another valid state. In other words, the data integrity constraints of the database must be maintained during any transaction. Data integrity rules such as unique keys, foreign keys, and check constraints are enforced during database transactions. Any violation of these constraints will cause the transaction to roll back. In real-world scenarios, we can consider a transaction in which an employee's new salary is updated to a specific amount, but the value entered is negative. Since negative salaries are impossible, the transaction would be rolled back.

- Isolation: Isolation protects transactions from one another. It means that each transaction should operate as if it were the only transaction executing in the database. The concept of isolation is critical when multiple users or applications access the same database simultaneously. In SQL Server, we specify the isolation level of our transaction using the SET TRANSACTION ISOLATION LEVEL statement. Some isolation levels include Read uncommitted, Read committed, Repeatable read, and Serializable. For instance, concurrent transactions that access the same data should not interfere with one another, which can result in data inconsistency. Ensuring isolation helps prevent data inconsistency by ensuring that transactions remain isolated and do not impact each other.

- Durability: Durability ensures that once a transaction is committed, the changes made persist even during system failures, power outages, or other catastrophic events. Durability is typically accomplished by logging the changes made by transactions in a transaction log (or other means), which is replayed during system recovery. For example, let's say a user purchases a product on an e-commerce website. The transaction is committed, but later, the server crashed due to a power outage. When the system restarts, the changes made during the transaction should be persisted in the database such that the database returns to the state it was in before the outage.

In summary, the ACID properties provide a consistent and reliable way of processing transactions that protect the integrity of the data in the database. They help to guarantee that transactions execute reliably and consistently, even under certain circumstances such as system failures. Understanding and implementing these basic concepts can significantly contribute to the robustness and reliability of a database.

3.6   What is a deadlock in SQL Server, and how can you resolve or prevent it?

A deadlock in SQL Server is a situation where two or more transactions are unable to proceed with their execution because they are holding locks on resources that the other transaction(s) need to complete. In other words, each transaction is waiting for the other transaction to release its lock on the needed resource, resulting in a standstill or "deadlock".

Here's an example scenario:

Transaction 1:

- Acquires a shared lock on Table A
- Requests an exclusive lock on Table B

Transaction 2:

- Acquires a shared lock on Table B
- Requests an exclusive lock on Table A

At this point, both transactions are waiting for the other to release its lock on the resource it needs to proceed, resulting in a deadlock.

To resolve or prevent a deadlock, you can take the following steps:

1. Identify the cause of the deadlock: Use SQL Server Profiler or system DMVs to capture information about the deadlock, such as the involved transactions, the resources they are holding locks on, and the timing of the deadlock. This information can help you identify the root cause of the deadlock.

2. Reduce the transaction duration: If transactions are taking too long to complete, they increase the chances of deadlocks. Try to break transactions into smaller batches that can complete quickly.

3. Use consistent transaction order: If your application always accesses resources in the same order, deadlocks can be avoided. For instance, if Transaction 1 always accesses Table A before Table B,

and Transaction 2 always accesses Table B before Table A, a dead-lock cannot occur.

4. Reduce transaction isolation level: If your application does not require high levels of isolation, you can reduce the isolation level to decrease the likelihood of deadlocks. For example, changing the isolation level from "SERIALIZABLE" to "READ COMMITTED" can help reduce deadlocks.

5. Use lock hints: Use lock hints like "TABLOCKX" or "HOLD-LOCK" to minimize the number of locks held on resources. Lock hints can help ensure that a transaction acquires all the necessary locks upfront, reducing the chances of deadlocks.

6. Implement retry logic: If a deadlock does occur, your application can be designed to retry the transaction. By implementing retry logic, your application can recover from a deadlock and proceed with its execution.

In summary, deadlocks can be resolved or prevented by identifying their root cause, reducing transaction duration, using consistent transaction order, reducing transaction isolation level, using lock hints, and implementing retry logic.

3.7 Can you explain the difference between a subquery and a correlated subquery?

In SQL Server, a subquery is a query that is nested inside another query and is executed first to produce a result set that is used by the outer query. On the other hand, a correlated subquery is a subquery that is related to the outer query such that it must be executed for each row processed by the outer query.

Let's look at an example to understand this difference.

Consider two tables: 'Sales' and 'Products'. 'Sales' table has the following columns: 'SaleID', 'ProductID', 'SaleDate', and 'SalePrice'. The 'Products' table has the following columns: 'ProductID', 'ProductName', 'ProductCost'.

To fetch all the sales records in which the sale price is greater than the average product cost, we can use a subquery as follows:

```
SELECT SaleID, ProductID, SaleDate, SalePrice
FROM Sales
WHERE SalePrice > (SELECT AVG(ProductCost) FROM Products)
```

In this query, the inner subquery '(SELECT AVG(ProductCost) FROM Products)' is executed first to calculate the average product cost. The result of this subquery is used to filter the records in the outer query.

Now, let's consider another example. Suppose we want to fetch all products whose product cost is less than the average cost of all products in the same product category. To achieve this, we need to use a correlated subquery. The query would look like this:

```
SELECT ProductID, ProductName, ProductCost
FROM Products p1
WHERE ProductCost < (SELECT AVG(ProductCost)
                     FROM Products p2
                     WHERE p1.ProductID = p2.ProductID)
```

In this query, the inner subquery '(SELECT AVG(ProductCost) FROM Products p2 WHERE p1.ProductID = p2.ProductID)' is correlated with the outer query by the condition 'p1.ProductID = p2.ProductID'. This means that the subquery needs to be executed for each row in the 'Products' table.

In summary, the main difference between a subquery and a correlated subquery is that a subquery is executed only once, whereas a correlated subquery is executed for each row processed by the outer query.

3.8   What is the purpose of the SQL Server Profiler, and how is it used?

SQL Server Profiler is a tool used for monitoring SQL Server instances. The purpose of SQL Server Profiler is to capture events that occur on a SQL Server instance and log them to a trace file. It is used for troubleshooting, auditing, and performance tuning.

SQL Server Profiler captures a wide range of events, such as SQL batches, stored procedure calls, and connection activity. It also captures performance data, including CPU usage, I/O usage, and memory usage. Profiler can be used to identify and diagnose issues related to slow-running queries, high CPU or I/O usage, and locking and blocking. It can also be used to track changes to the database, such as schema modifications and user permission changes.

To use SQL Server Profiler, follow these steps:

1. Open SQL Server Profiler.

2. Create a new trace by selecting the appropriate SQL Server instance and database.

3. Select the events to be captured in the trace.

4. Define filters to limit the data captured by the trace.

5. Start the trace and reproduce the issue or scenario of interest.

6. Stop the trace and review the captured data.

For example, to capture slow-running queries, the SQL:BatchCompleted event can be selected, and a filter can be applied to only capture queries with a duration greater than a certain threshold. The captured data can then be analyzed to identify the slow queries and tune them for better performance.

SQL Server Profiler can also be used in conjunction with other tools, such as Database Engine Tuning Advisor, to optimize database performance. The captured trace can be used as input to the tuning advisor, which will suggest indexes and other optimizations to improve query performance.

In summary, SQL Server Profiler is a powerful tool for monitoring and troubleshooting SQL Server instances. By capturing events and performance data, it can be used to diagnose issues and optimize database performance.

3.9   What is a cursor in SQL Server, and when should you use one?

A cursor is a database object that allows for iterative processing of a result set one row at a time. In SQL Server, a cursor is a temporary database object that can be used to retrieve and manipulate rows within a result set.

The primary use case for a cursor in SQL Server is when the result set requires more complex processing than can be achieved with standard SQL statements. For example, a cursor can be used to iterate through a subset of rows in a table while performing custom calculations or performing row-by-row updates.

While cursors can be useful in certain scenarios, they can also be expensive in terms of performance and resource utilization. Cursors often require additional memory allocation and may cause locking and blocking issues if not properly managed. It is generally recommended to avoid using cursors unless absolutely necessary.

Here is an example of how to use a cursor in SQL Server:

```
DECLARE @id INT
DECLARE @name VARCHAR(50)

DECLARE myCursor CURSOR FOR
SELECT id, name
FROM myTable

OPEN myCursor

FETCH NEXT FROM myCursor INTO @id, @name

WHILE @@FETCH_STATUS = 0
BEGIN
  -- Perform custom processing on the current row
  PRINT 'ID:␣' + CONVERT(VARCHAR, @id) + ',␣Name:␣' + @name

  FETCH NEXT FROM myCursor INTO @id, @name
END

CLOSE myCursor
DEALLOCATE myCursor
```

In this example, a cursor is used to retrieve rows from a table called 'myTable'. The 'FETCH NEXT' statement retrieves the next row in the result set, and the loop continues until all rows have been processed. The 'CLOSE' and 'DEALLOCATE' statements are used to release the resources used by the cursor.

3.10   How can you optimize a SQL Server query for better performance?

Optimizing SQL Server queries is important for improving database performance. There are different techniques that can be applied to optimize a SQL Server query for better performance. Here are some of them:

1. Use Indexes: Indexes are used to speed up data retrieval operations. The index reduces the number of rows that need to be scanned to retrieve data from the table. Indexes can be added on columns that are frequently used in queries to improve performance.

Example:

```
CREATE INDEX idx_lastname ON employees (lastname ASC)
```

2. Refactor queries: Complex queries can sometimes be simplified by breaking them down into simpler parts. This can help the optimizer to come up with a better execution plan.

Example:

```
SELECT a.lastname, a.firstname, b.orderdate
FROM employees a
JOIN orders b ON a.employeeid = b.employeeid
WHERE a.employeeid = 123 AND b.orderdate > '2021-01-01'
```

3. Use stored procedures: Stored procedures can improve performance by reducing network traffic between the database and the application. Stored procedures are compiled and stored in memory which makes them faster to execute.

Example:

```
CREATE PROCEDURE sp_getEmployeeOrders
  @employeeid INT,
  @orderdate DATE
AS
BEGIN
  SELECT a.lastname, a.firstname, b.orderdate
  FROM employees a
  JOIN orders b ON a.employeeid = b.employeeid
  WHERE a.employeeid = @employeeid AND b.orderdate > @orderdate
END
```

4. Use appropriate join types: Different join types can be used de-

pending on the relationship between tables. Inner join is the most
common type of join and is used when only matching rows are required.

Example:

```
SELECT a.lastname, a.firstname, b.orderdate
FROM employees a
JOIN orders b ON a.employeeid = b.employeeid
WHERE a.employeeid = 123 AND b.orderdate > '2021-01-01'
```

5. Avoid using SELECT *: SELECT * should be avoided as it can
lead to unnecessary scanning of columns that are not required. Query
only for columns that you are interested in.

Example:

```
SELECT lastname, firstname
FROM employees
WHERE employeeid = 123
```

6. Use table partitioning: Table partitioning breaks down large tables
into smaller more manageable parts. This can speed up queries that
only require data from a specific partition.

Example:

```
CREATE PARTITION FUNCTION pf_employee (INT)
AS RANGE LEFT
FOR VALUES (1000, 2000, 3000, 4000)

CREATE PARTITION SCHEME ps_employee
AS PARTITION pf_employee ALL TO ([PRIMARY])

CREATE TABLE employees
(
  employeeid INT,
  firstname VARCHAR(50),
  lastname VARCHAR(50),
  CONSTRAINT pk_employee PRIMARY KEY CLUSTERED (employeeid)
)
ON ps_employee(employeeid)
```

These are some of the techniques that can be used to optimize SQL
Server queries for better performance. However, optimization requires
careful analysis and testing of the queries and their impact on the
database.

3.11 What are the differences between the COMMIT, ROLLBACK, and SAVE-POINT commands in SQL Server?

In SQL Server, the COMMIT, ROLLBACK, and SAVEPOINT commands are used to manage transactions.

A transaction is a sequence of one or more SQL statements that are executed as a single unit of work. Transactions ensure that if one part of the sequence fails, the entire sequence is rolled back, and no changes are made to the database. The COMMIT, ROLLBACK, and SAVEPOINT commands let you control the boundaries of transactions.

Here are the details of each command:

1. COMMIT:
The COMMIT command is used to permanently save changes that have been made to the database within a transaction. If the transaction is successful, the data will be permanently saved. If the transaction is unsuccessful, the changes are rolled back, and the data is restored to its previous state.

Syntax:

```
COMMIT;
```

Example:

```
BEGIN TRANSACTION;
UPDATE employee SET salary=salary+5000 WHERE department_id=1;
COMMIT;
```

This transaction increases the salary of all employees in department 1 by 5000, and if the transaction is successful, it is permanently committed to the database.

2. ROLLBACK:
The ROLLBACK command is used to undo any changes made within a transaction. If the transaction fails or there is an error, you can use the ROLLBACK command to return the database to its previous state, undoing any changes that were made within the transaction.

Syntax:

```
ROLLBACK;
```

Example:

```
BEGIN TRANSACTION;
UPDATE employee SET salary=salary+5000 WHERE department_id=1;
IF @@ERROR <> 0
    ROLLBACK;
```

This transaction increases the salary of all employees in department 1 by 5000, but if there is any error, the entire transaction is rolled back, and the data is restored to its previous state.

3. SAVEPOINT:

The SAVEPOINT command is used to mark a point within a transaction to which you can later roll back. This allows you to undo a portion of a transaction that has already been committed.

Syntax:

```
SAVE TRANSACTION savepoint_name;
```

Example:

```
BEGIN TRANSACTION;
UPDATE employee SET salary=salary+5000 WHERE department_id=1;
SAVE TRANSACTION my_savepoint;
UPDATE employee SET salary=salary+5000 WHERE department_id=2;
IF @@ERROR <> 0
    ROLLBACK my_savepoint;

COMMIT;
```

This transaction increases the salary of all employees in department 1 by 5000 and saves a savepoint. Then, it increases the salary of all employees in department 2 by 5000, but if there is any error, only the changes made after the savepoint are rolled back, and the first update statement is still committed.

In summary,

```
- COMMIT command permanently saves changes made within a transaction in the
    database
- ROLLBACK command undo any changes made within a transaction and restores
    the data to a previous state
- SAVEPOINT command marks a point within a transaction that allows to roll
    back to later.
```

3.12 Can you describe the various types of replication in SQL Server?

In SQL Server, replication is the process of copying and distributing data and database objects from one database to one or more other databases. There are three types of replication supported in SQL Server:

1. Snapshot Replication:

Snapshot replication distributes a copy of the entire database or the specific objects at a specific moment in time to one or more subscribers. This type of replication is typically used for data warehouses or reference data that doesn't change frequently. In snapshot replication, the entire snapshot of the published database is copied over to the subscriber(s) at scheduled intervals.

When a snapshot is generated and delivered to a subscriber, the snapshot represents a completely independent copy of the original database. After that, changes made to the original database are not propagated to the subscriber unless a new snapshot is created and delivered.

2. Transactional Replication:

Transactional replication is used to keep copies of the data synchronized between the publisher and subscribers continuously. This type of replication is used in cases where the subscriber data needs to be updated soon after the publisher data is changed, and the subscriber data may be cached in memory for fast access.

Transactional replication works by tracking the changes made to the publisher database and forwarding those changes to the subscribers. A transactional replication system has three main components:

```
- Publisher: The database that provides the data and tables to replicate.
- Distributor: An application that moves the data between the publisher and
     the subscribers.
- Subscriber: The database that receives the replicated data.
```

3. Merge Replication:

Merge replication is used to replicate data between two or more SQL

Server databases and it is suited for applications where both the publisher and subscriber require updating the same data frequently but independently. In Merge replication, data is modified at both the publisher and subscribers.

In the case of conflicts, the changes made at the subscriber will have priority, and changes made on both sides are combined during synchronization. Merge replication requires at least one column in each table to uniquely identify a row, and all changes to the primary key values must be propagated to all subscribers.

In summary, SQL Server supports three types of replication to distribute data and database objects between different databases: Snapshot Replication, Transactional Replication, Merge Replication. The choice of the type of replication is crucial in determining the performance, maintenance and scalability of the database.

3.13   What is the difference between a temporary table and a table variable in SQL Server?

Temporary tables and table variables are two mechanisms to store and manipulate data within SQL Server, in general they work similarly but there are some differences between them.

Temporary tables are physical tables that are created in the tempdb database and their data is stored in disk pages, similar to regular tables. They can be created using the 'CREATE TABLE' statement with the '#' or '##' prefix to indicate that they are temporary. Temporary tables can be used to store data temporarily during a session, for instance to break down complicated queries into smaller steps or to store intermediate results. A temporary table can be accessed by multiple users simultaneously, as long as they are within the same session. Once the session ends, the temporary table is dropped and its data is removed from the tempdb database. Temporary tables can have indexes, constraints, and triggers like regular tables.

Table variables are basically variables that hold a table-level object, a table variable is used like a regular variable in Transact-SQL (T-SQL)

code, they don't require an explicit drop statement and their scope is
limited to the current batch, procedure, or trigger that created them.
Table variables store their data in memory, which makes them efficient for small to medium-sized datasets or when dealing with small
working sets, so table variables can be used when a temporary table
would be overkill. Table variables do not support indexes or constraints, so their data is accessed using table scans and they may
have poor performance if their size exceeds a certain limit (memory
pressure).

A basic comparison between them would be:

- Temporary Tables:

  - Data stored in 'tempdb' on disk.

  - Can be accessed by multiple sessions.

  - Can have indexes, constraints, and triggers.

  - Require explicit creation and removal.

  - Optimized for large data sets.

- Table Variables:

  - Data stored in memory.

  - Limited to the current batch or scope.

  - Do not support indexes or constraints.

  - Automatically cleaned up after use.

  - Optimized for small to medium-sized data sets.

Here is an example code showing how to use both of these concepts:

```
--Using Temporary Tables
USE AdventureWorks2019;
GO

CREATE TABLE #Temp
(
  ID int PRIMARY KEY,
  Name varchar(50)
);

INSERT INTO #Temp(ID, Name)
SELECT ProductID, Name
FROM Production.Product;

SELECT *
FROM #Temp
WHERE ID BETWEEN 50 AND 55;
```

```
DROP TABLE #Temp;
GO

--Using Table Variables
DECLARE @TableVar AS TABLE
(
  ID int PRIMARY KEY,
  Name varchar(50)
);

INSERT INTO @TableVar(ID, Name)
SELECT TOP 10 ProductID, Name
FROM Production.Product
ORDER BY ProductID;

SELECT *
FROM @TableVar
WHERE ID BETWEEN 50 AND 55;
```

In this code, we create a temporary table '#Temp' and store data
from the 'Production.Product' table in it. We then select a subset
of the data from '#Temp' based on a criterion before dropping the
table. In the second part of the code, we declare a table variable
'@TableVar' and store 10 rows from 'Production.Product' in it using
a 'SELECT' statement with an 'ORDER BY' clause. We then select
a subset of the data from '@TableVar' based on a criterion.

Overall, both temporary tables and table variables are useful tools
in SQL Server and each has its own strengths and weaknesses. The
choice between them depends on the specific requirements of the situation at hand.

3.14 Can you explain the use of the PIVOT and UNPIVOT operators in SQL Server?

PIVOT:
The PIVOT operator is used to rotate rows into columns resulting in
a summary table. This operator is useful in situations where the data
needs to be transformed from a row-based format to a column-based
format.

Example:

Consider a table called sales which has the following data:

```
| Product | Month | Sales |
```

```
|---------|-------|-------|
| Prod_1  | Jan   | 100   |
| Prod_1  | Feb   | 200   |
| Prod_1  | Mar   | 300   |
| Prod_2  | Jan   | 150   |
| Prod_2  | Feb   | 250   |
| Prod_2  | Mar   | 350   |
```

To represent this data in a column-based format with the products as the columns and the months as the rows, we can use the PIVOT operator as shown below:

```
SELECT Month, Prod_1, Prod_2
FROM
(
  SELECT Product, Month, Sales
  FROM sales
) src
PIVOT
(
  SUM(Sales)
  FOR Product IN (Prod_1, Prod_2)
) piv;
```

This will result in the following output:

```
| Month | Prod_1 | Prod_2 |
|-------|--------|--------|
| Jan   | 100    | 150    |
| Feb   | 200    | 250    |
| Mar   | 300    | 350    |
```

UNPIVOT:
The UNPIVOT operator is used to rotate columns into rows resulting in a normalized table. This operator is useful in situations where we need to transform column-based data to row-based data.

Example:

Consider a table called sales which has the following data:

```
| Month | Prod_1 | Prod_2 |
|-------|--------|--------|
| Jan   | 100    | 150    |
| Feb   | 200    | 250    |
| Mar   | 300    | 350    |
```

To represent this data in a row-based format with each row representing a product and a month, we can use the UNPIVOT operator as shown below:

```
SELECT Month, Product, Sales
FROM
(
  SELECT Month, Prod_1, Prod_2
  FROM sales
) src
UNPIVOT
(
  Sales FOR Product IN (Prod_1, Prod_2)
) unpiv;
```

This will result in the following output:

```
| Month | Product | Sales |
|-------|---------|-------|
| Jan   | Prod_1  | 100   |
| Jan   | Prod_2  | 150   |
| Feb   | Prod_1  | 200   |
| Feb   | Prod_2  | 250   |
| Mar   | Prod_1  | 300   |
| Mar   | Prod_2  | 350   |
```

In summary, PIVOT and UNPIVOT are powerful operators in SQL Server that allow us to transform data from row-based or column-based formats. These operators are especially useful in situations where we need to summarize or normalize data.

3.15   What is a Common Table Expression (CTE), and how is it used in SQL Server?

A Common Table Expression (CTE) is a temporary result set defined within the execution context of a single SELECT, INSERT, UPDATE, DELETE, or CREATE VIEW statement. It is similar to a derived table, but with some added benefits. CTEs can simplify and enhance the readability of SQL code by allowing for a more modular approach to composing complex queries.

Along with its readability benefits, this feature also provides the ability to recursively refer to the CTE within itself, which can be useful for complex hierarchical queries.

To create a CTE, we use the 'WITH' clause followed by a sequential definition of the CTEs. Each CTE is defined as a named subquery using a 'SELECT' statement, and these subqueries can refer to each

other or even to tables outside the CTEs. The syntax for creating a
CTE is as follows:

```
WITH cte_name (column_list)
AS
(
    SELECT ...
)
SELECT ...
```

Here, 'cte_name' is the name of the CTE, and 'column_list' is the
list of columns that the query returns for that CTE. The 'SELECT...'
statement can be any valid SQL query.

For example, here is a simple CTE that calculates the sum of all sales
by region:

```
WITH RegionSales (Region, TotalSales)
AS
(
    SELECT Region, SUM(Sales) AS TotalSales
    FROM Sales
    GROUP BY Region
)
SELECT * FROM RegionSales;
```

The above example creates a CTE called 'RegionSales' which sum-
marises the total sales for each region. The final 'SELECT' statement
retrieves the results from this CTE.

CTEs can also be used to write self-recursive queries. For example,
consider the following simple CTE that calculates the factorial of a
given number:

```
WITH RecursiveFactorial (n, Factorial)
AS
(
    SELECT 1, 1
    UNION ALL
    SELECT n+1, (n+1)*Factorial
    FROM RecursiveFactorial
    WHERE n < 10
)
SELECT n, Factorial FROM RecursiveFactorial;
```

Here, the CTE called 'RecursiveFactorial' uses a recursive query to
calculate the factorial of a given number. The 'UNION ALL' keyword
connects the anchor member (the base case, 'n' = 1 and 'Factorial' =
1) with the recursive member, and the 'WHERE' clause defines the
recursion termination condition ('n' < 10).

In conclusion, CTEs offer a powerful and flexible way to create modular and readable SQL code. They can be used to simplify the queries, enhance the readability of code, and even to handle complex scenarios such as self-recursion.

3.16   What is the difference between a scalar-valued and a table-valued user-defined function?

In SQL Server, user-defined functions (UDFs) are custom functions that can be created by users. They can be of two types - scalar-valued and table-valued. The difference between them lies in their purpose, return value, and usage.

A scalar-valued UDF returns a single scalar value (e.g. integer, string, etc.) as its result, based on the input parameters passed to it. It can be used in SELECT, WHERE or any other clause that requires a single value. For example, consider the following scalar-valued UDF that returns the length of a string input:

```
CREATE FUNCTION fn_GetStringLength(@str VARCHAR(50))
RETURNS INT
AS
BEGIN
    DECLARE @len INT
    SET @len = LEN(@str)
    RETURN @len
END
```

This UDF takes a string input parameter and returns its length as an integer value. It can be called in a query like this:

```
SELECT fname, lname, dbo.fn_GetStringLength(fname) AS fname_length
FROM employees
WHERE dbo.fn_GetStringLength(fname) > 5;
```

In this example, we use the scalar-valued UDF to calculate the length of the 'fname' column and use it in a WHERE clause to filter the results.

On the other hand, a table-valued UDF returns a table as its result, based on the input parameters passed to it. It can be used in FROM clause or JOIN clauses, like any other table. For example, consider the following table-valued UDF that returns all the products whose price is greater than a specified value:

```
CREATE FUNCTION fn_GetProductsByPrice(@price DECIMAL(18,2))
RETURNS TABLE
AS
RETURN
(
    SELECT * FROM products
    WHERE price > @price
);
```

This UDF takes a decimal input parameter and returns a table containing all the products whose price is greater than that value. It can be used in a query like this:

```
SELECT * FROM dbo.fn_GetProductsByPrice(100);
```

In this example, we use the table-valued UDF to get all the products whose price is greater than 100.

In summary, a scalar-valued UDF returns a single scalar value while a table-valued UDF returns a table. Scalar-valued UDFs are used in SELECT, WHERE, and other clauses that require a single value, whereas table-valued UDFs are used in FROM and JOIN clauses as if they were tables.

3.17   How can you implement error handling in SQL Server using TRY-CATCH blocks?

In SQL Server, error handling can be implemented using the TRY-CATCH block. The TRY-CATCH block provides a mechanism for handling and processing errors that occur in a SQL Server script.

The TRY-CATCH block consists of two parts: the TRY block and the CATCH block. The code within the TRY block is executed first. If an error occurs within the TRY block, SQL Server jumps to the CATCH block, where the error can be handled.

Here is the basic syntax of a TRY-CATCH block in SQL Server:

```
BEGIN TRY
   -- SQL code to execute
END TRY
BEGIN CATCH
   -- Error-handling code
END CATCH
```

Within the CATCH block, the error can be processed in a variety of ways. For example, the error message can be displayed to the user, the error can be logged to a file or database table, or the error can be passed up to the calling application.

Here is an example of how to use the TRY-CATCH block to handle a divide by zero error:

```
BEGIN TRY
   SELECT 10/0
END TRY
BEGIN CATCH
   PRINT 'Error:␣' + ERROR_MESSAGE()
END CATCH
```

In this example, the SELECT statement in the TRY block would normally result in a divide by zero error. However, the error is caught by the CATCH block, which displays the error message using the ERROR_MESSAGE function.

Another useful function within the CATCH block is the ERROR_NUMBER function, which returns the error number associated with the error that occurred.

```
BEGIN TRY
   SELECT 10/0
END TRY
BEGIN CATCH
   PRINT 'Error␣number:␣' + CAST(ERROR_NUMBER() as varchar(10))
END CATCH
```

In this example, the ERROR_NUMBER function is used to display the error number associated with the divide by zero error.

Overall, the TRY-CATCH block provides a flexible and powerful way to implement error handling in SQL Server scripts, and it is essential for creating robust and reliable database applications.

3.18   What are the differences between the ROW_NUMBER(), RANK(), and DENSE_RANK() functions in SQL Server?

ROW_NUMBER(), RANK(), and DENSE_RANK() are three different functions in SQL Server that are used to generate a sequence of unique values based on a given column's order.

ROW_NUMBER()

ROW_NUMBER() function generates consecutive integers for each row of the result set. It assigns a unique value to each row within the partition specified in the OVER() clause. Partitioning divides the result set by one or more columns or expressions specified in the PARTITION BY clause. If PARTITION BY is not specified, the whole result set is treated as a single partition.

The syntax for the ROW_NUMBER() function is:

```
ROW_NUMBER() OVER ( PARTITION BY <column_name> ORDER BY <column_name> )
```

Here is an example of the ROW_NUMBER() function:

```
SELECT ROW_NUMBER() OVER(ORDER BY sales) AS RowNumber, * FROM sales_table
```

This query will return the sales table with a new column called RowNumber which will be the row number of each row based on the sales column in ascending order.

RANK()

RANK() function assigns a value to each row within the partition based on the ordinal position of the row within the result set. The rank of the first row is 1, the rank of the second row is 2, and so on. If there are ties, then multiple rows will receive the same rank, and the subsequent rank will be skipped.

The syntax for the RANK() function is:

```
RANK() OVER ( PARTITION BY <column_name> ORDER BY <column_name> )
```

Here is an example of the RANK() function:

```
SELECT RANK() OVER(PARTITION BY country ORDER BY sales DESC) AS Rank, * FROM
    sales_table
```

This query will return the sales table with a new column called Rank, which will assign a rank to each country based on their sales in descending order.

DENSE_RANK()

DENSE_RANK() function is similar to the RANK() function, but if there are ties, the same rank is not skipped. This function assigns a unique rank to each distinct value within the partition based on their order in the result.

The syntax for the DENSE_RANK() function is:

```
DENSE_RANK() OVER ( PARTITION BY <column_name> ORDER BY <column_name> )
```

Here is an example of the DENSE_RANK() function:

```
SELECT DENSE_RANK() OVER(ORDER BY sales) AS Rank, * FROM sales_table
```

This query will return the sales table with a new column called Rank, which will assign a dense rank to each row based on the sales column in ascending order.

In conclusion, the ROW_NUMBER() function assigns unique values to distinct rows in a partition, regardless of the presence of ties, while the RANK() and DENSE_RANK() functions assign unique values to each distinct value in a partition, with RANK() skipping ranks in the presence of ties and DENSE_RANK() not skipping ranks.

3.19   What is the purpose of the SQL Server Agent, and what are its main components?

The SQL Server Agent is a Microsoft SQL Server component that is responsible for automating tasks such as backups, database maintenance, and running scheduled jobs. In other words, it allows for automation of routine tasks that can be scheduled to run at specified times or after specific events.

The main components of the SQL Server Agent are:

1. Jobs: A SQL Server Agent job is a set of one or more tasks that are grouped together as a single unit of work. A job can include tasks such as running a script, executing a database query, or sending an email notification.

2. Schedules: A schedule determines when a job is executed. A SQL Server Agent job can be scheduled to run at specific intervals (such as every hour or every day) or at specific times (such as 3:00 AM on Saturdays).

3. Alerts: Alerts can be created to send notifications when specific events occur. For example, an alert can be configured to send an email notification if a job fails to complete successfully.

4. Operators: An operator is a person or group of people who receive notifications when alerts are triggered. For example, an operator can be notified by email or pager when a job fails to complete successfully.

5. Proxies: A proxy is a security principal that enables job steps to run under a different security context than the SQL Server Agent service account. This allows more precise security control for job execution.

The SQL Server Agent is an essential component for automating routine tasks in SQL Server environments. It provides a centralized tool for scheduling and executing jobs, sending notifications, and managing security for job execution.

3.20   Can you explain the role of SQL Server Integration Services (SSIS) in data integration and transformation?

SQL Server Integration Services (SSIS) is a powerful tool provided by Microsoft that enables data integration and transformation. It is a platform for building high-performance data integration and workflow solutions that extract, transform, and load (ETL) data from various sources into a target system.

The primary role of SSIS in data integration is to provide a tool that is flexible, efficient, and easy to use. It provides a visual interface that allows users to design and deploy complex ETL processes without having to write a single line of code. With SSIS, we can extract data from various sources, transform it based on specific business rules, and load it into a target system such as a data warehouse, a data mart, or a relational database.

SSIS supports a wide range of data sources, including flat files, Excel spreadsheets, XML documents, and ODBC-compliant databases such as SQL Server, Oracle, and MySQL. It also supports a variety of data formats, including CSV, TXT, and DTS.

SSIS incorporates a wide range of transformation tools that can be used to manipulate the data as it flows through the ETL process. Examples of transformations include filtering, sorting, merging, and aggregating data. In addition, SSIS provides powerful tools for data cleansing, such as deduplication, formatting, and standardizing.

Another key role of SSIS is to provide advanced features that make it possible to build complex ETL workflows. For example, it provides a rich set of control flow tasks that can be used to build complex workflows that involve conditional execution, looping, and error handling. It also supports package configurations, which allow us to dynamically configure package properties based on runtime values, making it possible to build highly flexible and customizable ETL processes.

In summary, SQL Server Integration Services is a powerful and flexible tool that plays a critical role in data integration and transformation. It provides a wide range of features that enable us to extract, transform, and load data from virtually any source into any target system.

With SSIS, data integration and transformation processes can be designed, tested, and deployed quickly and easily, making it an essential tool for any organization that needs to manage large amounts of data.

Chapter 4

Advanced

4.1 What is the difference between a star schema and a snowflake schema in data warehousing?

In data warehousing, a star schema and a snowflake schema are two common ways to model the relationships between tables. Both schemas are used to organize data for efficient querying and analysis.

In a star schema, there is one central fact table that contains the core data that is being analyzed. This fact table is surrounded by dimension tables, each of which contains a specific category of attributes related to the core data. Each dimension table is connected to the fact table through a foreign key relationship. The fact table contains numerical measures, such as sales or profits, whereas the dimension tables contain descriptive attributes, such as time, geography, or product details.

In contrast, a snowflake schema is a variation of a star schema where the dimension tables are further normalized. This means that some dimension tables are broken up into additional dimension tables, creating a more complex and detailed schema. For example, a dimension table for products may have separate tables for categories and subcategories. This results in a more normalized schema that can be more flexible and maintainable, but potentially slower to query due to the additional tables and relationships.

In summary, a star schema is a simpler, denormalized schema that is easier to understand and query, while a snowflake schema is a more complex, normalized schema that is more flexible and maintainable. Choosing between the two depends on the specific needs of the data warehouse and the trade-off between simplicity and flexibility.

4.2 How can you use SQL Server's dynamic management views (DMVs) and dynamic management functions (DMFs) to troubleshoot performance issues?

SQL Server's dynamic management views (DMVs) and dynamic management functions (DMFs) provide valuable insight into the internal workings of SQL Server, and these insights can be an important part of troubleshooting performance issues.

DMVs and DMFs are specialized views and functions that expose detailed information about SQL Server's internal state. DMVs are a set of system views that provide real-time information regarding server health, and DMFs are system functions that accept parameters, perform an action, and return a table that can be used in a query.

DMVs can be queried using Transact-SQL (T-SQL), and DMFs can be used in the SELECT statement to provide additional information. Both DMVs and DMFs are designed to provide real-time information, so they can be used to identify performance bottlenecks and other issues that may impact SQL Server's ability to perform.

For example, the sys.dm_exec_query_stats DMV can be used to identify queries that are consuming the most resources. By examining the query_plan column, you can identify the source of the problem and make any necessary adjustments to optimize the query.

```
SELECT TOP 10
  SUBSTRING(qt.TEXT, (qs.statement_start_offset/2)+1, (
      (CASE qs.statement_end_offset
```

```
        WHEN -1 THEN DATALENGTH(qt.TEXT)
        ELSE qs.statement_end_offset
        END - qs.statement_start_offset)/2)+1),
    qs.execution_count,
    qs.total_worker_time/qs.execution_count AS average_cpu_time,
    qs.total_elapsed_time/qs.execution_count AS average_elapsed_time,
    qs.total_logical_reads/qs.execution_count AS average_logical_reads,
    qs.total_logical_writes/qs.execution_count AS average_logical_writes,
    qs.total_physical_reads/qs.execution_count AS average_physical_reads,
    qs.creation_time,
    qs.last_execution_time,
    qp.query_plan
FROM sys.dm_exec_query_stats qs
CROSS APPLY sys.dm_exec_sql_text(qs.sql_handle) qt
CROSS APPLY sys.dm_exec_query_plan(qs.plan_handle) qp
ORDER BY qs.total_worker_time DESC;
```

Another example is the sys.dm_os_wait_stats DMV. By examining this DMV, you can identify which wait types are causing SQL Server to wait the longest, which can help you identify performance bottlenecks.

```
SELECT TOP 10 wait_type,
       waiting_tasks_count,
       wait_time_ms,
       max_wait_time_ms
FROM sys.dm_os_wait_stats
ORDER BY wait_time_ms DESC;
```

In addition to DMVs and DMFs, SQL Server also provides several other performance monitoring tools, including SQL Server Profiler and Extended Events. When used in combination with DMVs and DMFs, these tools can help you diagnose and resolve performance issues, and ensure that your SQL Server environment is running at peak performance.

4.3   Can you explain the concept of parameter sniffing and how it affects query performance in SQL Server?

Parameter sniffing refers to the process by which SQL Server generates an execution plan based on the parameter values passed to a stored procedure or query. When a stored procedure or query is executed for the first time, SQL Server generates an execution plan based on the parameter values passed to it. This execution plan is then cached for subsequent executions of the stored procedure or query that use the same parameter values.

Parameter sniffing can significantly improve query performance, as SQL Server can optimize the execution plan to take advantage of the specific parameter values being passed. However, it can also lead to performance issues in some cases.

When the parameter values passed to a stored procedure or query vary widely, SQL Server may generate a suboptimal execution plan based on the initial parameter values used. For example, if a stored procedure is designed to return all employees who have worked for the company for more than five years, but is called with a parameter value of '1' (which represents employees who have worked for the company for one year), SQL Server may generate an execution plan that is optimized for returning a small number of rows, which may be inefficient when applied to a larger dataset.

Similarly, if the dataset being queried is highly skewed, with a few outliers having significantly different characteristics from the majority of the data, the execution plan generated by parameter sniffing may not be optimal for the outliers.

To address these issues, SQL Server provides a number of options for managing parameter sniffing, including:

1. The OPTION (OPTIMIZE FOR) query hint, which allows you to specify a specific parameter value to optimize the execution plan for.

2. The OPTION (OPTIMIZE FOR UNKNOWN) query hint, which tells SQL Server to generate an execution plan that is optimized for a typical parameter value.

3. Parameter masking, which involves creating a copy of the parameter value within the stored procedure or query and using the copy instead of the original parameter value to generate the execution plan.

4. Dynamic SQL generation, which involves generating the SQL statement dynamically based on the parameter values passed at runtime, rather than using a precompiled stored procedure or query.

It's important to note that parameter sniffing is just one factor that can affect query performance in SQL Server, and that there are many other factors to consider when optimizing a database. Nonetheless, understanding the concept of parameter sniffing and how it can impact performance is an important part of designing and maintaining efficient database systems.

4.4 What is the role of SQL Server Analysis Services (SSAS) in business intelligence and analytics?

SQL Server Analysis Services (SSAS) is a crucial component in the Microsoft Business Intelligence stack. It is used to create and manage online analytical processing (OLAP) cubes, which provide a fast and efficient way for users to slice and dice large amounts of data. Analysis Services utilizes the data from SQL Server databases and other data sources to create a multidimensional view of your data, allowing for easy exploration and analysis.

SSAS has several key roles in business intelligence and analytics:

1. Data modeling: SSAS allows for the creation of complex data models that can handle millions of rows of data. Using tools like the Cube Wizard, developers can create hierarchies, measures, and calculated members that provide a clear picture of the data.

2. Aggregation: SSAS includes built-in algorithms for aggregating data over multiple dimensions. This is particularly useful for handling large volumes of data quickly, allowing for near-instantaneous querying and analysis of data.

3. Data mining: SSAS provides data mining capabilities for discovering patterns and relationships in data. This can be used for a variety of purposes, such as predictive analytics, customer segmentation, and fraud detection.

4. Reporting: SSAS integrates with other Microsoft BI tools like Power BI, Excel, and SQL Server Reporting Services to create powerful reports and dashboards. This allows organizations to make data-driven decisions quickly and easily.

Overall, SSAS plays a critical role in enabling business intelligence and analytics by providing fast, efficient access to large amounts of data in a multidimensional format. It allows developers and analysts to model, analyze, and report on data in a way that is intuitive and easy to use.

4.5 How do you configure and manage database mirroring in SQL Server for high availability and disaster recovery?

Database mirroring in SQL Server is a high-availability and disaster-recovery solution that provides data redundancy and failover capability in case of a database failure. It involves creating and managing a mirrored copy of a database on another server, known as the mirror server. The process of configuring and managing database mirroring can be divided into the following steps:

1. Prerequisites: Ensure that both the principal and mirror servers are running the same edition of SQL Server, have the same collation, and are connected to the same network. Also, make sure that the databases involved in mirroring are in the Full recovery model.

2. Setting up endpoints: Database mirroring requires setting up endpoints, which are network sockets that allow communication between the principal and mirror servers. The endpoints can be configured using either T-SQL or SQL Server Management Studio. You can create the endpoints using the following T-SQL command:

```
CREATE ENDPOINT endpoint_name
STATE = STARTED
AS TCP (LISTENER_PORT = endpoint_port, LISTENER_IP = ALL)
FOR DATABASE_MIRRORING (ROLE = PARTNER)
```

Replace endpoint_name with a name for the endpoint, endpoint_port with the port number for the endpoint, and PARTNER with either PARTNER or WITNESS, depending on the role of the server.

3. Initializing the mirror database: To initialize the mirror database, take a full backup of the principal database and restore it on the mirror server with the NORECOVERY option. Then, take a transaction

log backup of the principal database and restore it on the mirror server with the NORECOVERY option. Finally, restore any subsequent transaction log backups with the NORECOVERY option. You can use the following T-SQL command to restore the backups:

```
RESTORE DATABASE database_name
FROM DISK = 'backup_file_name'
WITH NORECOVERY
```

Replace database_name with the name of the database, backup_file_name with the name of the backup file, and NORECOVERY with the appropriate option.

4. Starting mirroring: After setting up endpoints and initializing the mirror database, you can start mirroring using T-SQL or SQL Server Management Studio. To start mirroring using T-SQL, run the following command on the principal server:

```
ALTER DATABASE database_name
SET PARTNER = 'TCP://mirror_server:port'
```

Replace database_name with the name of the database and mirror_server:port with the endpoint of the mirror server.

5. Testing failover: Once mirroring is set up and running, you should test failover to ensure that it works as expected. To initiate a failover manually, use the following T-SQL command on the principal server:

```
ALTER DATABASE database_name
SET PARTNER FAILOVER
```

Replace database_name with the name of the database.

In conclusion, database mirroring in SQL Server is a powerful high-availability and disaster-recovery solution that can help ensure that critical data remains available in case of a failure. The process of configuring and managing database mirroring involves setting up endpoints, initializing the mirror database, starting mirroring, and testing failover. By following these steps, you can create a robust mirroring solution that provides data redundancy and failover capability for your organization.

4.6   What is the difference between a login and a user in SQL Server security?

In SQL Server security, a login is a principal that allows access to the SQL Server instance as a whole, while a user is a principal that allows access to a specific database within the instance.

A login is used to authenticate a user's connection to the SQL Server instance. It consists of a set of credentials, such as a username and password, or a Windows account, that are validated by the SQL Server instance.

On the other hand, a user is a database-level principal that has a particular set of permissions within a database. A user is created based on the login used to connect to the SQL Server instance. Each login can be associated with one or more database users, and each user is associated with only one login.

Here is an example of creating a login and a user:

```
CREATE LOGIN [testlogin] WITH PASSWORD=N'testpass'
GO
USE [testdb]
GO
CREATE USER [testuser] FOR LOGIN [testlogin]
GO
```

In this example, the 'CREATE LOGIN' statement creates a login with the name 'testlogin' and a password of 'testpass', and the 'CREATE USER' statement creates a database user with the name 'testuser' for that login in the 'testdb' database.

It is important to note that a login can have access to multiple databases within the SQL Server instance, but a user only has access to the specific database it is created in.

In summary, a login is used to authenticate access to the SQL Server instance, while a user is used to grant access to a specific database within the instance.

4.7 Can you explain the use of the SQL Server FileStream feature for handling large binary objects (BLOBs)?

SQL Server FileStream feature provides an efficient way of storing and managing large binary objects (BLOBs) in a SQL Server Database. FileStream enables the data to be stored on the file system rather than being directly saved in the database, which makes it ideal for handling large BLOBs that can consume a lot of database storage and memory resources.

When the FileStream feature is enabled on a SQL Server, it creates a special type of file group called FileStream File Group. This file group is used to store the BLOB data as a collection of files outside the database. These files are then accessed through a special type of SQL Server column called the FileStream column.

To illustrate the use of SQL Server FileStream, let's consider an example of storing images in a database. Traditionally, storing images in a database would involve creating a SQL Server column of type VARBINARY(MAX) to hold the image data. This approach soon becomes impractical when dealing with a large number of images because it consumes a lot of memory and storage resources. In contrast, using the FileStream feature makes it easy to manage large images in the database.

To use FileStream, you need to configure the SQL Server instance to support FileStream, create a FileStream file group, and add a FileStream column to the table where you want to store the data. The following T-SQL script shows how to create a table with a FileStream column:

```
CREATE TABLE Images
(
    ImageID int PRIMARY KEY,
    ImageDescription varchar(50),
    ImageData varbinary(max) FILESTREAM
)
```

Notice how we use "FILESTREAM" as the data type for the Image-Data column. This tells SQL Server to store the large binary data outside the database file on the file system. The FileStream data can then be accessed using the special FileStream API in Transact-SQL or through .NET programming.

By using the FileStream feature to store BLOBs, we can take advantage of the file system features for managing large files, such as backup and recovery, file compression, and remote storage. FileStream also provides better performance for inserting, updating, and retrieving large binary data compared to traditional methods of storing BLOB data in SQL Server columns.

In conclusion, the FileStream feature in SQL Server provides a robust and efficient way of storing and managing large binary objects in a database. By using FileStream, you can take advantage of file system features for managing large files and achieve better database performance when working with BLOB data.

4.8 What is the role of SQL Server Reporting Services (SSRS) in creating and managing reports?

SQL Server Reporting Services (SSRS) is a powerful tool used for creating, managing, and delivering reports in a variety of formats. The primary role of SSRS is to provide a platform for creating and delivering reports based on data from SQL Server and other data sources.

SSRS offers a wide range of features and capabilities, including:

1. Report design: SSRS allows for the creation of highly customizable reports with an intuitive drag-and-drop interface that includes multiple data visualization options such as charts, tables, maps, and gauges.

2. Data sources and connections: SSRS allows for the connection to multiple data sources, including SQL Server, Oracle, and other databases. SSRS also supports connecting to flat files, OLE DB and ODBC data sources.

3. Data aggregation and filtering: SSRS enables users to aggregate data based on specific requirements and to filter the data to include

only the necessary information.

4. Delivery and scheduling: SSRS allows for scheduling of report delivery via email and other mechanisms. Reports can be saved in a variety of formats including PDF, Excel, and Word.

5. Security and access control: SSRS provides robust security features to control access to reports and data sources. Administrators can set up role-based security to control who has access to reports and the data within them.

6. Report caching: SSRS provides an option to cache reports, which can help reduce server load and improve performance.

Overall, SSRS plays an important role in creating and managing reports, as it provides a flexible platform for working with data, visualizing results, and delivering reports in a variety of formats. SSRS is a well-known reporting tool in the industry, and it provides a high degree of control and security to its users.

4.9 How do you use Extended Events in SQL Server for monitoring and performance analysis?

Extended Events in SQL Server is a powerful tool used for the collection of diagnostic and performance data of SQL Server. It enables database administrators to monitor and capture events in real-time with lightweight performance overhead.

In SQL Server, several event classes are already defined, and administrators can use these event classes to observe the behavior of the system. However, using Extended Events, administrators can create custom event sessions that are tailored to specific monitoring requirements.

Here are the steps to create an Extended Event session in SQL Server:

1. Launch the SQL Server Management Studio (SSMS), connect to the SQL Server instance, and expand the Management node.

2. Right-click the Extended Events folder and select the New Session Wizard to launch the Create New Session Wizard.

3. Enter the name of the new event session, select the event source, and configure the event details.

4. Define the events and data you want to capture by adding event modules to the event session.

5. Specify the actions to be taken when the events occur, such as writing the event data to a file or sending an email notification.

6. Set the session event filter and other advanced configurations.

7. Start the session, and monitor the events as they occur.

One of the significant advantages of using Extended Events is that it consumes minimal system resources and has a low overhead. A well-designed Extended Event session can provide meaningful insights into the performance of a SQL Server instance with negligible performance impact.

For example, suppose we wish to monitor the T-SQL Statements executed on a specific database. In that case, we can create a new session, configure the event details, and add the SQL statement event module to the session. Here's what the script would look like:

```
CREATE EVENT SESSION [TSQL Tracing] ON SERVER
ADD EVENT sqlserver.sql_statement_completed(
    ACTION(sqlserver.sql_text,sqlserver.tsql_stack)
    WHERE ([database_name]='MyDatabase'))
ADD TARGET package0.asynchronous_file_target(
    SET filename='C:ExtendedEventLogsTSQLTracing.xel',
    metadatafile='C:ExtendedEventLogsTSQLTracingMetadata.xem'
    )
WITH (MAX_DISPATCH_LATENCY=5 SECONDS)
GO

ALTER EVENT SESSION [TSQL Tracing] ON SERVER STATE=START;
```

In this example, we have created a new event session to capture completed SQL statements executed on the "MyDatabase" database. The event data is written to an asynchronous file target located at "C:/ExtendedEventLogs/". We have also set the maximum dispatch latency to 5 seconds, which defines the maximum time it may take for events to be dispatched to the target.

In conclusion, Extended Events are a powerful tool for monitoring and performance analysis in SQL Server. By designing well-crafted event sessions, we can capture relevant events and data with negligible performance overhead, leading to improved system performance and user experience.

4.10   What is partitioning in SQL Server, and how can it improve query performance?

Partitioning is the process of logically dividing a large table into smaller, more manageable partitions or filesgroups, while maintaining the appearance of a single large table, partitioning allows you to increase SQL Server performance.

Partitioning can improve query performance in several ways:

1. Reduced query execution time: When a table is partitioned, SQL Server can quickly prune the partitions that do not contain the required data, resulting in much faster query execution.

2. Parallelism: By using partitioning with a well-designed indexing strategy, SQL Server can take advantage of parallelism, allowing multiple processors or threads to work on different partitions simultaneously, thereby improving overall query performance.

3. Easier maintenance: Partitioning also makes maintenance tasks such as backups, index rebuilds or defragmentations faster and easier since they can be done on individual partitions rather than the entire table.

4. Better data management: Partitioning can also improve data management by allowing you to move or archive old data to separate filegroups or storage devices for better data organization and faster access to frequently used data.

Here's an example of how partitioning can be used to improve query performance:

Suppose you have a large table containing sales transactions from the past several years with millions of rows. Instead of querying the entire table every time, you can partition the table by year, with each year's data placed in a separate partition.

Then, when you run a query to retrieve sales data for a specific year, SQL Server can quickly scan only the partition for that year, drastically reducing query execution time compared to a full table scan.

To implement partitioning in SQL Server, you need to choose a partitioning key (such as date, ID, or location), create a partition function that defines the ranges of values for each partition, and then bind the partition function to the table or index.

The following is an example of how to create a partition function that partitions a table by date in SQL Server:

```
CREATE PARTITION FUNCTION DateRangePF (datetime)
AS RANGE LEFT FOR VALUES
('20200101', '20210101', '20220101')
```

This code creates a partition function called 'DateRangePF' that partitions data based on the date. It creates three partitions in the table based on the ranges of values passed in the 'FOR VALUES' clause.

After creating the partition function, you can then create a partition scheme which associates it with a specific filegroup:

```
CREATE PARTITION SCHEME DateRangePS
AS PARTITION DateRangePF
TO (PRIMARY, FG2019, FG2020, FG2021)
```

The schema 'DateRangePS' maps the partitions to different filegroups - based on the year of transactions - so that data can be managed more efficiently.

Finally, you can alter your table or index to use the partition scheme:

```
ALTER TABLE sales
DROP CONSTRAINT PK_sales_sfid
WITH (MOVE TO ZB2019)

ALTER TABLE sales
ADD CONSTRAINT PK_sales_sfid
PRIMARY KEY CLUSTERED (salesforceid, transactiondate)
ON DateRangePS (transactiondate)
```

This code alters a table 'sales' to use the partition scheme ('DateRangePS') and creates a clustered index with a partition key of the 'transactiondate' column. The primary key and clustered index are also moved from the original filegroup ('PRIMARY') to the parti-

CHAPTER 4. ADVANCED   91

tion scheme filegroups ('FG2019', 'FG2020'and 'FG2021) to improve performance.

In summary, partitioning is a powerful technique that can greatly improve query performance, especially for large tables with millions of rows. By using partitioning in combination with other optimization techniques such as indexing, query optimization, and parallelism, you can achieve even greater performance gains.

4.11 What are the best practices for index maintenance in SQL Server to optimize performance?

Indexes play a crucial role in optimizing SQL Server performance, and index maintenance is an essential task for maintaining the database performance. Index maintenance in SQL Server refers to the process of monitoring and rebuilding indexes to ensure that they are optimized efficiently.

Here are some best practices for index maintenance in SQL Server:

1. Index Fragmentation: Index fragmentation occurs when a table's records are updated, deleted or inserted, leading to unused space in index pages. The unused space in the index pages causes the index to become scattered, leading to slower query performance. It's essential to regularly monitor the indexes to identify any fragmentation and use SQL Server in-built functionality such as Index Fragmentation Report or DMV sys. dm_db_index_physical_stats to identify the index status.

2. Index Rebuild: Index rebuilding involves dropping and recreating the index, which can be time-consuming and resource-intensive. Hence, it's essential to monitor the index's fragmentation before deciding whether to rebuild the index. If an index has more than 30

3. Index Reorganization: Index reorganization is a lighter weight alternative to index rebuilding. Index reorganization is useful when the index fragmentation is less than 30

4. Fill Factor: The fill factor is a setting that defines how much free space to leave within each data page. It's essential to set the correct fill factor depending on the table's characteristics and expected insert/update/delete activity. When the fill factor is too low, excessive fragmentation is likely to occur. When too high, disk space is wasted, and reading from the index may take longer.

5. Index Columns: Choosing the correct columns for an index is key to optimization. A good index should contain the most selective columns, leading to beneficial query performance. A bad index contains multiple columns, such as the Primary Key, leading to decreased query performance.

6. Maintenance Plan: Consider setting up SQL Server Maintenance Plan to perform regular index optimization, including both rebuild and reorganization.

To summarize, index maintenance in SQL Server requires regular attention to ensure optimum query performance. Consider monitoring system fragmentation levels, rebuilding damaged indexes, and exercising caution while performing rebuilds of clustered indexes. Determine which columns to include in an index thoughtfully, and consider scheduling maintenance plans.

4.12 Can you explain the difference between a full-text index and a standard index in SQL Server?

A standard index in SQL Server is used to speed up queries that involve searching for specific values in one or more columns of a table. It organizes the data in a way that allows the database engine to find the desired values more quickly than if it had to scan the entire table. A standard index can be created on one or more columns of a table and can be clustered or nonclustered.

On the other hand, a full-text index is used to speed up queries that involve searching for words or phrases within a large amount of text data stored in a table. It allows for sophisticated text-based searches that can handle linguistic variations such as stemming, synonyms, and inflectional forms. A full-text index can be created on a single column or multiple columns of a table and is always nonclustered.

Both types of indexes help improve query performance, but they serve different purposes. A standard index is ideal for tables with small to medium amounts of data that are queried using exact matches, while a full-text index is better suited for large amounts of text data that require complex searches.

Here's an example of how to create a standard index on a table in SQL Server:

```
CREATE INDEX idx_customer_name ON customers (last_name, first_name);
```

This creates a nonclustered index on the 'last_name' and 'first_name' columns of the 'customers' table.

And here's an example of how to create a full-text index on a table in SQL Server:

```
CREATE FULLTEXT INDEX idx_product_description ON products(description
    LANGUAGE 1033);
```

This creates a nonclustered full-text index on the 'description' column of the 'products' table, with language ID 1033 (U.S. English).

4.13 How do you implement Transparent Data Encryption (TDE) in SQL Server to secure data at rest?

Transparent Data Encryption (TDE) is a feature in SQL Server that enables encryption of the database files at rest. With TDE, you can protect sensitive data such as credit card information, social security numbers, and proprietary information in case your database files are stolen, hacked, or misplaced.

To enable TDE in your SQL Server database, follow these steps:

1. Create a master key:

```
USE master;
CREATE MASTER KEY ENCRYPTION BY PASSWORD = '<password>';
```

Here, you are creating a master key that will be used to protect the
encryption key.

2. Create a certificate:

```
CREATE CERTIFICATE MyServerCert
WITH SUBJECT = 'My Server Certificate';
```

This certificate will be used to protect the encryption key.

3. Backup the certificate:

```
BACKUP CERTIFICATE MyServerCert TO FILE = '<path>'
WITH PRIVATE KEY (FILE = '<path>', ENCRYPTION BY PASSWORD = '<password>');
```

This step is important as you need to keep a copy of the certificate in
a safe location. The certificate will be used to decrypt the encryption
key in case of server failure.

4. Create a database encryption key:

```
USE <database>;
CREATE DATABASE ENCRYPTION KEY
WITH ALGORITHM = AES_256
ENCRYPTION BY SERVER CERTIFICATE MyServerCert;
```

Here, you are creating a database encryption key that will be used
to encrypt the data in your database. The key is protected by the
certificate you created earlier.

5. Turn on encryption:

```
ALTER DATABASE <database> SET ENCRYPTION ON;
```

Finally, you turn on encryption for your database.

After following these steps, your database encryption key is encrypted
with the server certificate, which is protected by the master key. Your
entire database, including table data, indexes, and temporary files, is
encrypted at rest.

It is important to note that TDE does not protect data in transit,
such as when it is being transmitted from an application to the server

or from one server to another. For that, you would need to use other encryption methods such as SSL/TLS.

4.14 What is the AlwaysOn Availability Groups feature in SQL Server, and how does it ensure high availability and disaster recovery?

The AlwaysOn Availability Groups feature in SQL Server is a high availability and disaster recovery solution that provides a combination of database-level high availability and disaster recovery. It is a feature introduced in SQL Server 2012 to replace the Database Mirroring feature which is now deprecated.

AlwaysOn Availability Groups work by creating a group of SQL Server databases that failover together. The database group consists of a primary replica and one or more secondary replicas, which can be located on separate servers or in separate data centers. The primary replica is responsible for the read-write workload, while the secondary replica(s) can be used to offload read-only workloads and improve database performance.

In case of a failure of the primary replica, the database group automatically fails over to the secondary replica, ensuring continuity of service without data loss. The failover process is automatic and can be configured to be synchronous or asynchronous depending on the level of data protection required. When synchronous mode is used, the secondary replica acknowledges receipt of the transaction before the primary replica commits the transaction to the database, ensuring zero data loss during failover. On the other hand, asynchronous mode can be used when the latency between primary and secondary replicas is high, and some degree of data loss is acceptable during failover.

AlwaysOn Availability Groups also provide disaster recovery solutions through the use of an offsite replica called a secondary replica. This replica is kept in a different location than the primary replica and can be used to quickly recover from regional disasters such as earthquakes,

floods, or hurricanes. In addition, backups taken on the secondary
replica can be used to restore the database in case of a complete
failure of the primary replica.

AlwaysOn Availability Groups can also be combined with other SQL
Server features such as Windows Failover Clustering, backups, and
log shipping to provide a complete solution for high availability and
disaster recovery.

For example, consider a global e-commerce website with customer
data stored in a SQL Server database. The website must be available
24/7 as even a short downtime can have significant financial implications. The AlwaysOn Availability Groups feature can be used here
to create a database group consisting of a primary replica and several secondary replicas. The primary replica can be used to handle
the read-write workload, while the secondary replicas can be used to
offload read-only workloads and improve database performance.

In addition, a failover cluster can be configured with multiple nodes
to provide high availability for the SQL Server instance hosting the
primary replica. This ensures continuity of service in case of hardware
or software failures on any of the nodes.

Finally, backups taken on a secondary replica can be used to restore
the database in case of a complete failure of the primary replica.
Overall, this combined solution ensures high availability and disaster
recovery for the e-commerce website's SQL Server database.

4.15   How can you use Resource Governor in SQL Server to manage resource allocation and improve performance?

Resource Governor is a feature introduced in SQL Server 2008 that
helps manage resource allocation and improve performance by allowing the administrator to limit and prioritize resource usage. It allows
for the classification of workloads into resource pools and then allocates resources to those pools based on defined limits and priorities.

To use Resource Governor, the first step is to create resource pools

for various workloads according to their priority and resource requirements. Resource pools can be created using the following T-SQL
code:

```
CREATE RESOURCE POOL [pool_name]
WITH (
    max_memory_percent = xx,
    max_cpu_percent = xx,
    min_cpu_percent = xx
)
```

where 'pool_name' is the name of the resource pool, 'max_mem-
ory_percent' is the maximum amount of memory that can be allocated by the pool, 'max_cpu_percent' is the maximum percentage
of CPU that can be used by the pool, and 'min_cpu_percent' is the
minimum percentage of CPU that must be allocated to the pool.

Once the resource pools are created, the next step is to create workload groups and associate them with the appropriate resource pool.
Workload groups are created using the following T-SQL code:

```
CREATE WORKLOAD GROUP [group_name]
USING [pool_name]
```

where 'group_name' is the name of the workload group and 'pool_name'
is the name of the associated resource pool.

The final step is to classify incoming connections into the appropriate
workload group. This can be done using classifier functions, which
are user-defined functions that take user-defined inputs and return
the name of the workload group to which the connection belongs.

One example of a classifier function is based on the login name of the
connection. The following T-SQL code creates a classifier function
that assigns connections with login names starting with "admin" to
the high-priority workload group:

```
CREATE FUNCTION [dbo].[fn_classifier]()
RETURNS SYSNAME
WITH SCHEMABINDING
AS
BEGIN
    DECLARE @workload_group_name SYSNAME
    IF (SUSER_NAME() LIKE 'admin%')
        SET @workload_group_name = 'high_priority_group'
    ELSE
        SET @workload_group_name = 'default_group'

    RETURN @workload_group_name
END
```

Finally, the classifier function must be associated with the Resource Governor configuration using the following T-SQL code:

```
ALTER RESOURCE GOVERNOR
WITH (CLASSIFIER_FUNCTION=[dbo].[fn_classifier])
```

Resource Governor can also be used to limit the number of concurrent queries by using the 'MAX_DOP' option. This limits the number of processors used for parallel query execution.

In summary, Resource Governor is a powerful feature in SQL Server that can be used to manage resource allocation and improve performance by creating resource pools, workload groups, and classifier functions. By properly managing resource allocation, Resource Governor can help prevent runaway queries from monopolizing system resources and causing overall degradation of system performance.

4.16   What are the various types of constraints in SQL Server, and how do they help maintain data integrity?

Constraints are used to enforce rules and restrictions on the data stored in a database. In SQL Server, there are several types of constraints that can be used to maintain data integrity.

1. Primary Key Constraint: A primary key is a unique identifier for a row in a table. A primary key constraint ensures that each row in a table has a unique value for the primary key column. For example, consider a table named Employees with columns EmployeeID (primary key), Name, and Salary. The primary key constraint on the EmployeeID column ensures that each employee has a unique ID, which is used to identify them in the table.

2. Foreign Key Constraint: A foreign key is a column in a table that refers to the primary key of another table. A foreign key constraint ensures that the values in the foreign key column exist in the primary key column of the referenced table. For example, consider two tables named Orders and Customers. The Orders table has a foreign key column named CustomerID that refers to the primary key column of

the Customers table. The foreign key constraint on the Orders table ensures that a customer must exist in the Customers table before an order can be placed for that customer.

3. Unique Constraint: A unique constraint ensures that each value in a column is unique in a table. Unlike a primary key constraint, a unique constraint can contain null values. For example, consider a table named Books with columns BookID, Title, and ISBN. The ISBN column can have a unique constraint, which ensures that each book in the table has a unique ISBN.

4. Check Constraint: A check constraint is used to limit the values that can be inserted into a column. The check constraint is based on a Boolean expression that evaluates to true or false. For example, consider a table named Students with columns StudentID, Name, and Age. The check constraint on the Age column can limit the values to only those that are greater than or equal to 18.

5. Not Null Constraint: A not-null constraint ensures that a column does not contain null values. For example, consider a table named Orders with columns OrderID, CustomerID, and OrderDate. The not-null constraint on the CustomerID column ensures that every order has a customer associated with it.

These constraints ensure that data entered into the database is accurate, consistent, and valid. They help to maintain data integrity by preventing duplicate or invalid data from being entered into a table. This, in turn, helps to ensure the accuracy of reports and analyses performed on the data.

For example, consider an online shopping website that uses a database containing a table for orders. If the database did not have a foreign key constraint for the customerID column in the orders table, it would be possible to place an order without a customer associated with it. This would lead to inaccurate reporting of customer orders, and cause problems with fulfillment and shipping. However, the foreign key constraint ensures that all orders are associated with a valid customer, which helps to maintain data integrity.

4.17   How can you use SQL Server's Query Store feature to monitor and troubleshoot query performance?

SQL Server's Query Store is a powerful feature that can be used to monitor and troubleshoot query performance. It provides a way to capture and store query performance data (such as execution plans, run-time statistics, and execution history) over time, which can be used to identify and troubleshoot performance issues.

Here are some steps to using Query Store to monitor and troubleshoot query performance:

1. Enable Query Store - To enable Query Store for a database, simply execute the following command:

```
ALTER DATABASE [database_name] SET QUERY_STORE = ON;
```

2. Configure Query Store settings - Configure Query Store to collect the necessary data to monitor query performance by setting options like data retention (how long to store data), capture mode (to capture all queries or only those that cause performance issues), and query store size.

3. Monitor query performance - Query Store provides several built-in reports that you can use to monitor query performance, such as the Top Resource-Consuming Queries report, the Regressed Queries report, and the Query Store Overall Resource Consumption report. These reports can be accessed via SQL Server Management Studio (SSMS) or by using T-SQL queries.

4. Troubleshoot performance issues - Query Store allows troubleshooting of performance issues by identifying queries that are consuming a high amount of resources. The built-in reports available in Query Store can be used to identify queries with high average CPU usage, high average duration, or high IO usage, which can then be further analyzed to identify performance issues.

5. Analyze query execution plans - Query Store provides a way to view the execution plans of the queries that were executed in the past, which can be used to identify issues like plan changes or plan

regressions that are causing performance issues.

For example, here's a T-SQL query that can be used to identify the top 10 resource-consuming queries in Query Store:

```
SELECT TOP 10
  qt.query_sql_text,
  qsp.*
FROM
  sys.query_store_query_text AS qt
  JOIN sys.query_store_plan AS qsp ON qt.query_text_id = qsp.query_text_id
ORDER BY
  qsp.cpu_time DESC;
```

Overall, Query Store is a powerful tool that can be used by SQL Server Database expert to monitor and troubleshoot query performance issues, aiding them in identifying and resolving issues that may be detrimental system's overall performance.

4.18 What is the purpose of SQL Server Configuration Manager, and what can it be used for?

SQL Server Configuration Manager is a tool for managing the services that make up SQL Server. It is used to configure the settings of SQL Server services installed on a machine, including the SQL Server Database Engine, SQL Server Reporting Services, SQL Server Analysis Services and others associated with it.

With SQL Server Configuration Manager, administrators can view and change the configuration of SQL Server services that include setting log on or log off accounts, configuring server protocols, configuring network protocols and managing other settings. For instance, it is possible to view and change the authentication mode, configure port numbers and set up SSL certificates using the configuration manager.

Additionally, SQL Server Configuration Manager can be used to manage and configure the client protocols, such as Shared Memory, Named Pipes, TCP/IP, and VIA. By configuring these protocols, it is possible to establish network communications between a client and SQL Server.

SQL Server Configuration Manager can also be used to manage the SQL Server browser service, which is required when you run, among others, dynamic port mapping of named instances or clustering algorithms that use named instances.

In summary, SQL Server Configuration Manager is a feature-rich tool for managing and configuring different SQL Server services on one or more servers that run Windows. It is an essential tool for SQL Server administrators, especially those who manage complex and large database environments.

4.19   Can you explain the concept of columnstore indexes in SQL Server and their benefits?

Columnstore indexes are an important feature of SQL Server that were introduced in SQL Server 2012. They provide a new way of storing and querying data that can lead to substantial performance improvements for certain types of queries.

A columnstore index is a type of index that organizes the data in a table based on the values in a specific column or set of columns. Instead of storing the data in row format, columnstore indexes store the data in a column format. This can be especially beneficial for large tables with lots of columns, as it enables more efficient data compression and faster data retrieval for certain types of queries.

The main benefits of using columnstore indexes in SQL Server are:

1. Improved query performance: Columnstore indexes can speed up certain types of queries by allowing SQL Server to read and process only the columns that are needed for a particular query. This can reduce overall I/O and CPU usage, resulting in faster query response times.

2. Better data compression: Columnstore indexes use highly efficient compression algorithms that can significantly reduce the amount of disk space required to store large tables. This can help to reduce storage costs and improve overall database performance.

3. Increased throughput: Because columnstore indexes allow SQL Server to process large amounts of data quickly, they can help to improve throughput for certain types of queries. This means that more users can access and work with the database simultaneously without experiencing delays or performance issues.

Here is an example of creating a clustered columnstore index:

```
CREATE CLUSTERED COLUMNSTORE INDEX MyColumnstoreIndex
ON MyTable
```

Once the columnstore index is created, SQL Server will automatically determine when to use it for certain queries. It's important to note that not all types of queries will benefit from columnstore indexes, so it's recommended to test query performance before and after creating a columnstore index to ensure that it's actually improving performance.

In conclusion, columnstore indexes are a powerful feature of SQL Server that can help to improve query performance, reduce storage costs, and increase throughput for certain types of queries. However, they should be used carefully and selectively, as they may not be beneficial for all types of queries and tables.

4.20   What are the different types of SQL Server authentication modes, and how do you choose between them?

There are two different types of SQL Server authentication modes:

1. Windows authentication mode

2. Mixed mode

1. Windows authentication mode:
In Windows authentication mode, a user's Windows login is used to authenticate their identity. This mode is more secure because it ensures that only authenticated Windows users can access the SQL Server. Also, Windows Authentication is the default authentication mode, and the preferred mode for most applications.

2. Mixed mode:
In mixed mode, users can authenticate with either Windows or SQL
Server authentication, providing more flexibility. In this mode, Windows authentication is still the default and preferred authentication
method, but SQL Server authentication allows for username and
password-based authentication as well.

Choosing between authentication modes largely depends on the security requirements of your application. If your application is housed in
a secure, on-premises environment, Windows authentication mode is
generally the recommended choice due to its enhanced security features. In contrast, if you have a hybrid or cloud environment, or if
you need to support users who are not part of your domain, mixed
mode authentication may be necessary.

To configure authentication mode in SQL Server Management Studio,
follow these steps:

1. Connect to the SQL Server instance using an account with appropriate
permissions.

2. Right-click the instance name and select Properties.

3. Click Security under Select a page.

4. Choose the desired authentication mode and click OK to apply changes.

Here's an example of using T-SQL to check the current authentication
mode:

```
SELECT SERVERPROPERTY('IsIntegratedSecurityOnly');
```

This will return a value of 1 if Windows authentication mode is currently enabled or 0 if mixed mode is enabled.

Chapter 5

Expert

5.1 How does SQL Server handle lock escalation, and what are its potential drawbacks?

Lock escalation is a process in which a database management system (DBMS) changes a large number of fine-grained locks (e.g., row or page-level locks) to coarser-grained locks (e.g., table-level locks) to enhance performance.

SQL Server uses a lock escalation process to reduce the overhead of managing large numbers of fine-grained locks. When a transaction acquires locks on many rows or pages in a table or index, the lock manager may escalate the locks to a coarser granularity, such as at the table or partition level. This is because managing many fine-grained locks can consume significant system resources and also increase the overhead of the locking mechanism itself.

SQL Server uses two types of lock escalation:

1. **Automatic lock escalation**: happens automatically when the number of locks held by a single statement or transaction reaches a threshold. By default, this threshold is set to 5000 locks on a

single table or partition, or when the memory used for locks exceeds a
certain percentage of the available memory. Automatic lock escalation
happens in the background, and the system decides when and how to
escalate locks based on the workload and other system conditions.

2. **Manual lock escalation**: can be triggered by application code
or by a database administrator using the ALTER TABLE statement.
This allows the DBA to escalate locks at the table, partition or index
level as needed, though it is not commonly used.

The potential drawbacks of lock escalation include:

1. **Blocking**: Lock escalation can cause more blocking of resources
and concurrent queries. When locks are escalated to a higher level,
a single lock can affect more data, which can lead to queries waiting for locks to be released. This can result in performance issues,
particularly in high-concurrency environments.

2. **Reduced concurrency**: Escalating locks to the table or partition level can reduce concurrency, as a single lock can block multiple requests. This can lead to increased contention and decreased
throughput.

3. **Deadlocks**: Lock escalation can increase the likelihood of deadlocks, particularly in scenarios where multiple transactions are accessing the same table or partition.

4. **Memory usage**: Lock escalation can increase the memory used
by the lock manager. If too many locks are escalated too often, it can
lead to memory pressure on the system as a whole, potentially leading
to decreased performance or even out-of-memory errors.

In summary, SQL Server's lock escalation feature is intended to optimize the system's performance by reducing the overhead of managing
large numbers of fine-grained locks. However, lock escalation may
also cause issues such as blocking, reduced concurrency, deadlocks,
and increased memory usage. It is important for database administrators and developers to monitor the system's behavior and adjust
the lock escalation thresholds as needed to optimize performance for
their specific workloads.

5.2 What is the process of creating and managing a SQL Server failover cluster instance for high availability?

Creating and managing a SQL Server failover cluster instance involves the following steps:

1. Setting up the Windows Server Failover Cluster (WSFC): Before setting up the SQL Server Failover Cluster Instance (FCI), first, you need to create a WSFC, which is a group of servers that work together to manage and provide high availability for clustered resources. To set up a WSFC, you need at least two physical servers running a Windows Server operating system.

2. Meeting the prerequisites: Before installing SQL Server onto an FC instance, you need to meet specific hardware and software requirements. These requirements include having a storage area network (SAN), installing the appropriate networking protocols, enabling domain name system (DNS) resolution, installing the failover clustering feature, and creating domain accounts for SQL Server services.

3. Installing SQL Server FCI: After meeting the prerequisites, install SQL Server onto the WSFC by selecting the "Installation" option from the SQL Server setup menu. During installation, you need to select the "SQL Server Failover Cluster Instance" option, provide the virtual network name (VNN) of the instance, and specify the service accounts running the SQL Server services.

4. Configuring SQL Server FCI: After installing SQL Server on each node, configure the SQL Server instance. The configuration process involves creating a SQL Server administrator account, defining the instance name and network settings, setting up disk and storage configuration, and configuring the filestream feature.

5. Testing and managing the SQL Server FCI: Once the SQL Server FCI is installed, tested, and configured, it is essential to monitor the instance and manage it regularly. Regular management tasks include modifying the configuration settings, monitoring the available storage space, configuring backup, and testing failover capabilities.

6. Performing failover: In the event of a hardware or software fail-

ure on the active node, the WSFC automatically fails over the SQL
Server FCI to the passive node. This process ensures that an in-
stance is available, reducing downtime and ensuring high availability.
To perform a manual failover or troubleshoot issues with SQL Server
FCI, you can use the WSFC Manager interface or PowerShell cmdlets.

In summary, creating and managing a SQL Server FCI involves setting up a WSFC, meeting the prerequisites, installing SQL Server,
configuring the instance, testing and managing the FCI, and performing failover as necessary.

5.3 Can you explain the concept of buffer pool extension in SQL Server, and how it improves performance?

In SQL Server, a buffer pool is a region of memory used to cache data
pages, allowing for faster access and retrieval of data. However, in
some cases, the size of the buffer pool may not be sufficient, leading
to performance issues such as increased I/O activity and slower query
execution times.

To address this issue, SQL Server introduced the concept of a buffer
pool extension in SQL Server 2014. A buffer pool extension allows
the buffer pool to be augmented with memory from a non-volatile
storage device such as a solid-state drive (SSD), providing additional
memory for data page caching.

The buffer pool extension works by using a file that serves as an
extension to the buffer pool. The file is created on the SSD and
added to the buffer pool as a non-uniform memory access (NUMA)
node. The buffer pool can then use the memory allocated from the
SSD to cache additional data pages.

One advantage of using a buffer pool extension is that it can reduce
I/O bottlenecks and improve query performance. With a larger buffer
pool, more data pages can be stored in memory, reducing the need to
read data from disk. This can result in faster query execution times
and overall database performance.

An important consideration when using a buffer pool extension is
the type of storage device used. Solid-state drives (SSDs) are recommended for their high performance and low latency, which can
improve the effectiveness of the buffer pool extension. However, it
is important to ensure that the SSD has sufficient capacity to store
the buffer pool extension file and that it is configured properly for
optimal performance.

Here is an example of enabling a buffer pool extension in SQL Server:

```
-- Create a file on the SSD for the buffer pool extension
ALTER SERVER CONFIGURATION SET BUFFER POOL EXTENSION ON (FILENAME = 'F:
    SSDbuffer_pool_extension_file.ssd', SIZE = 100GB);

-- Add the file to the buffer pool as a NUMA node
ALTER SERVER CONFIGURATION SET NUMA CONFIGURATION ADD FILE (FILENAME = 'F:
    SSDbuffer_pool_extension_file.ssd', SIZE = 100GB);
```

In summary, a buffer pool extension is a useful feature in SQL Server
that can help improve database performance by providing additional
memory for data page caching. It is important to carefully consider
the type and configuration of the storage device used for the buffer
pool extension to ensure optimal performance.

5.4 How do you implement and manage SQL Server Service Broker for asynchronous messaging and distributed transactions?

SQL Server Service Broker is a message-based communication system
built into the SQL Server Database Engine. Applications can use it
to easily and reliably send and receive messages between different
SQL Server instances, databases, and even language platforms. It
also supports distributed transactions, making it a suitable choice for
implementing reliable and scalable asynchronous messaging solutions.

Here are the steps to implement and manage SQL Server Service
Broker for asynchronous messaging and distributed transactions:

1. Enable Service Broker: Before you can use Service Broker, you
need to enable it on the databases where you want to use it. To do

that, execute the following T-SQL command:

```
ALTER DATABASE [DatabaseName] SET ENABLE_BROKER;
```

2. Create message types: Message types define the format and structure of the messages that can be sent and received by Service Broker endpoints. You can create message types using the following T-SQL command:

```
CREATE MESSAGE TYPE [MessageType]
VALIDATION = NONE;
```

For example, the following command creates a message type called "OrderMessage" with the "XmlSchema" message format:

```
CREATE MESSAGE TYPE [OrderMessage]
VALIDATION = NONE
FORMAT = XML
XmlSchema('<xs:schema xmlns:xs="http://www.w3.org/2001/XMLSchema"/>');
```

3. Create contracts: Contracts define the message types that can be exchanged between Service Broker endpoints. You can create contracts using the following T-SQL command:

```
CREATE CONTRACT [ContractName]
([MessageType] SENT BY [Sender]
[, [MessageType] SENT BY [Sender]]*);
```

For example, the following command creates a contract called "OrderContract" that allows the "OrderMessage" message type to be sent by the "OrderSender" endpoint:

```
CREATE CONTRACT [OrderContract]
(OrderMessage SENT BY INITIATOR);
```

4. Create queues: Queues hold the messages sent and received by Service Broker endpoints. You can create queues using the following T-SQL command:

```
CREATE QUEUE [QueueName];
```

For example, the following command creates a queue called "OrderQueue":

```
CREATE QUEUE [OrderQueue];
```

5. Create services: Services define the endpoints for Service Broker communication. You can create services using the following T-SQL command:

```
CREATE SERVICE [ServiceName]
ON QUEUE [QueueName]
([ContractName]);
```

For example, the following command creates a service called "Order-Service" that uses the "OrderQueue" queue and the "OrderContract" contract:

```
CREATE SERVICE [OrderService]
ON QUEUE [OrderQueue]
([OrderContract]);
```

6. Send messages: You can send messages using the following T-SQL command:

```
SEND ON CONVERSATION [ConversationHandle]
MESSAGE TYPE [MessageType]
([MessageBody]);
```

For example, the following command sends an "OrderMessage" to the "OrderService" endpoint:

```
DECLARE @conversationHandle UNIQUEIDENTIFIER;
BEGIN DIALOG @conversationHandle
FROM SERVICE [OrderSender]
TO SERVICE 'OrderService' ON CONTRACT [OrderContract];

SEND ON CONVERSATION @conversationHandle
MESSAGE TYPE [OrderMessage]
('<Order><ProductId>1</ProductId><Quantity>10</Quantity></Order>');
```

7. Receive messages: You can receive messages using the following T-SQL command:

```
RECEIVE TOP(1)
CONVERT([DataType], [MessageBody]) AS [MessageBody]
FROM [QueueName];
```

For example, the following command receives a message from the "OrderQueue" queue:

```
DECLARE @messageBody NVARCHAR(MAX);

RECEIVE TOP(1)
CONVERT(NVARCHAR(MAX), [MessageBody]) AS [MessageBody]
FROM [OrderQueue];

SELECT @messageBody;
```

8. Handle transactions: Service Broker supports distributed transactions, which allow multiple operations across multiple databases and servers to be treated as a single atomic transaction. To start a new transaction, you can use the BEGIN TRANSACTION statement. To commit or rollback a transaction, you can use the COMMIT TRANSACTION or ROLLBACK TRANSACTION statement.

For example, the following command starts a new transaction and sends a message using Service Broker:

```
BEGIN TRANSACTION;

DECLARE @conversationHandle UNIQUEIDENTIFIER;
BEGIN DIALOG @conversationHandle
FROM SERVICE [OrderSender]
TO SERVICE 'OrderService' ON CONTRACT [OrderContract];

SEND ON CONVERSATION @conversationHandle
MESSAGE TYPE [OrderMessage]
('<Order><ProductId>1</ProductId><Quantity>10</Quantity></Order>');

COMMIT TRANSACTION;
```

If an error occurs, you can roll back the transaction using the ROLLBACK TRANSACTION statement:

```
BEGIN TRANSACTION;

DECLARE @conversationHandle UNIQUEIDENTIFIER;
BEGIN DIALOG @conversationHandle
FROM SERVICE [OrderSender]
TO SERVICE 'OrderService' ON CONTRACT [OrderContract];

SEND ON CONVERSATION @conversationHandle
MESSAGE TYPE [OrderMessage]
('<Order><ProductId>1</ProductId><Quantity>10</Quantity></Order>');

SELECT 1/0; -- cause an error

ROLLBACK TRANSACTION;
```

In addition to the above steps, managing Service Broker involves monitoring the queues, services, and endpoints to ensure that they are running smoothly and handle any issues that arise. You can use the sys.transmission_queue, sys.dm_broker_queue_monitors, and sys.dm_broker_activated_tasks system views to monitor Service Broker activity. You can also use the ALTER ENDPOINT, ALTER QUEUE, and ALTER SERVICE statements to modify existing Service Broker objects.

5.5 What are the best practices for SQL Server capacity planning and hardware sizing?

Capacity planning and hardware sizing are important considerations for SQL Server performance and scalability. It is essential to ensure that the hardware and resources allocated are sufficient to support the workload of the database. Below are some best practices for SQL Server capacity planning and hardware sizing:

1. Understand the workload: Before making any capacity planning or hardware sizing decisions, it is important to understand the workload of the database. This includes the size of the database, the number of users, the type of application, and the types of queries that are executed.

2. Plan for growth: It is important to plan for future growth when sizing hardware and capacity. This includes considering the expected growth rate of the database, as well as any future application or user requirements.

3. Choose the right hardware: The hardware chosen for SQL Server should be able to handle the workload of the database. This includes the number of CPUs, amount of RAM, and storage capacity. It is important to choose hardware that is scalable, so that it can be upgraded as the workload increases.

4. RAID configuration: RAID (Redundant Array of Independent Disks) can improve performance and provide redundancy in the event of disk failure. It is important to choose the right RAID configuration based on the workload of the database.

5. Use SSDs for storage: Solid State Drives (SSDs) can significantly improve SQL Server performance, compared to traditional hard drives. SSDs are faster at random access, which is important for databases that have a lot of random reads and writes.

6. Virtualization: Virtualization can be used to optimize hardware utilization, which can reduce costs. However, it is important to ensure that the virtual environment can support the workload of the database.

7. Monitor performance: Regularly monitoring SQL Server performance can help identify any hardware or capacity issues. This includes measuring CPU utilization, memory usage, and disk I/O performance.

Here is an example SQL script to get basic performance metrics from SQL Server:

```
SELECT
    GETDATE() AS [Date and Time],
    cpu.time_ticks / CONVERT(FLOAT, cpu.cntr_value) AS [CPU usage %],
    mem.cntr_value / 1024 AS [Memory usage (MB)],
    disk.cntr_value / 1024 AS [Disk I/O usage (MB/s)]
FROM
    sys.dm_os_performance_counters cpu
    INNER JOIN sys.dm_os_performance_counters mem ON cpu.object_name = mem.
        object_name
    INNER JOIN sys.dm_os_performance_counters disk ON cpu.object_name = disk.
        object_name
WHERE
    cpu.counter_name = 'Processor Time' AND
    cpu.instance_name = '_Total' AND
    mem.counter_name = 'Target Server Memory (KB)' AND
    mem.instance_name = '[Default]' AND
    disk.counter_name = 'Disk Read Bytes/sec' AND
    disk.instance_name = '_Total'
```

This SQL script will return the CPU usage percentage, memory usage in MB, and disk I/O usage in MB/s. These metrics can be used to identify any hardware or capacity issues and make necessary adjustments.

5.6   Can you explain the concept of indexed views in SQL Server, and what are the benefits and limitations?

Indexed views in SQL Server are virtual tables that are derived from a query on one or more base tables. The results of the query are stored in the view, just like a table, but the data is not physically stored. However, indexed views come with some additional features such as indexes and constraints which can help to increase the performance of complex queries.

The benefits of using indexed views include:

- Improved query performance: Indexed views can significantly improve the
    performance of queries that access large amounts of data or involve
    complex joins and aggregations. Since the view results are precomputed
    and stored, the query engine can retrieve the data much faster than if
    it had to compute it on the fly every time the query is executed.
- Reduced storage requirements: Since indexed views store the precomputed
    results of a query, they can often require less storage space than the
    equivalent query result set.
- Simplified query design: Indexed views can simplify the design of complex
    queries by precomputing the results of expensive joins and aggregations,
    making the query simpler and more efficient to execute.
- Enhanced security: Indexed views can be used to restrict access to
    sensitive data, by limiting the columns exposed through the view.

However, there are some limitations to using indexed views as well:

- Maintenance overhead: Indexed views require additional maintenance overhead
    , as changes to the underlying tables may require the view to be
    refreshed or rebuilt, which can be time-consuming.
- Limited support for certain query constructs: Indexed views have some
    limitations on the types of queries they can support, such as the
    inability to use certain keywords like DISTINCT or GROUP BY or aggregate
    functions in a correlated subquery.
- Increased storage requirements: Depending on the size of the indexed view
    and the number of indexes created on it, the storage required for the
    view can be considerable, especially in scenarios where the view is
    updated frequently.

Here is an example of a basic indexed view definition:

```
CREATE VIEW [dbo].[MyIndexedView]
WITH SCHEMABINDING
AS
SELECT [Column1], [Column2], SUM([Column3]) as [TotalColumn3]
FROM [dbo].[MyTable]
GROUP BY [Column1], [Column2]
GO

CREATE UNIQUE CLUSTERED INDEX [MyIndexedView_index] ON [dbo].[MyIndexedView
    ]([Column1], [Column2])
```

In this example, the indexed view is created based on a query that
sums the values in 'Column3' by grouping on 'Column1' and 'Col-
umn2' from the 'MyTable' table. The 'WITH SCHEMABINDING'
option ensures that the underlying table schema cannot be changed,
which is required for indexed views. A unique clustered index is created on the view to support faster retrieval of data.

To sum up, indexed views can be a powerful tool for improving query
performance and simplifying query design in SQL Server, but they do
come with overhead that needs to be considered carefully, especially
in scenarios where the underlying data changes frequently.

5.7   How do you plan and implement a disaster recovery strategy for a SQL Server environment?

Planning for a disaster recovery strategy for a SQL Server environment starts with understanding the criticality of the databases and the expectations of the business. It includes an analysis of the potential impact of downtime, recovery time objectives (RTO), and recovery point objectives (RPO).

Below are the steps to plan and implement a disaster recovery strategy for a SQL Server environment:

1. Create a Backup Strategy: The first step is to create a backup strategy. This ensures that in the event of a disaster, you have a copy of the data to restore from. There are various backup options available in SQL Server such as Full, Differential, and Transaction Log backups. Determine the retention period for backups and automate the backup process. It is also recommended to store a copy of the backups offsite for disaster recovery purposes.

2. High Availability Options: The next step is to implement high availability options. This includes options such as Always On Availability Groups, Database Mirroring, and Log Shipping. These options provide redundancy and failover capabilities in case of a disaster. Select the appropriate high availability option based on the criticality of the databases and the RPO and RTO objectives.

3. Disaster Recovery Site: Implement a Disaster Recovery (DR) site. The DR site should be in a remote location away from the production site to minimize the impact of a regional disaster. The DR site should have the same hardware and software as the production site to ensure the same level of performance.

4. Test the Plan: After implementing the disaster recovery plan, it is essential to test the plan regularly. This involves performing a full-scale disaster recovery simulation to ensure that the plan works as intended. Plan testings should be performed at least annually.

5. Update the Plan: A disaster recovery plan is not a one-time activity. This plan should be reviewed and updated regularly as the

business, environment, and technologies change. Identify the changes that are required, such as adding new databases or implementing new technologies.

In conclusion, a disaster recovery plan is critical to ensure business continuity in case of a disaster. A well-designed disaster recovery plan includes a backup strategy, high availability options, a disaster recovery site, testing the plan, and updating the plan regularly.

5.8   How can you use the SQL Server Data Quality Services (DQS) for data cleansing and matching?

SQL Server Data Quality Services (DQS) is a data quality and data cleansing tool provided by Microsoft. DQS can be used for data cleansing, matching, and profiling.

Data cleansing is the process of identifying and correcting or removing inaccurate, incomplete, or irrelevant data. Data matching is the process of identifying duplicate or similar records within a dataset. DQS provides both functionalities to ensure that data is accurate and consistent.

To use DQS for data cleansing and matching, you need to follow the following steps:

1. Create a DQS knowledge base: A knowledge base is a repository of data and rules that DQS uses to match and cleanse data. You can create a new knowledge base or use an existing one.

2. Define domains: A domain is a set of values that are valid for a given attribute. A domain can be used to validate and normalize data. You can define domains for each attribute in your dataset.

3. Define rules: A rule is a condition that data must comply with to be considered valid. Rules can be used to identify and correct errors in your data. You can define rules for each domain in your knowledge base.

4. Create a DQS project: A project is a container for data cleansing and matching tasks. You can create a new project or use an existing one.

5. Import data: You can import data into DQS from a variety of sources, including SQL Server, Excel, and CSV files.

6. Perform data profiling: Data profiling is the process of analyzing data to identify quality issues. DQS provides profiling tools that can be used to identify missing values, invalid data, and other problems.

7. Cleanse data: DQS provides several cleansing tools that can be used to correct errors in data. For example, the Replace tool can be used to replace one value with another, while the Trim tool can be used to remove leading and trailing spaces.

8. Match data: DQS provides several matching algorithms that can be used to identify duplicate or similar records within a dataset. For example, the Exact Match algorithm can be used to identify records that have the same values in all attributes, while the Fuzzy Grouping algorithm can be used to identify records that have similar values in some attributes.

9. Export data: Once you have cleaned and matched your data, you can export it to a variety of formats, including SQL Server, Excel, and CSV files.

In summary, DQS provides a comprehensive set of tools for data cleansing and matching. By following the above steps, you can use DQS to ensure that your data is accurate and consistent.

5.9 What are the different types of database snapshots in SQL Server, and how can they be used in different scenarios?

In SQL Server, a snapshot is a read-only copy of a database at a fixed point in time. There are two types of database snapshots in SQL Server:

1. **Database snapshot**: A database snapshot is a point-in-time, read-only copy of an entire database. It is created from an existing database and allows users to query the data as it existed at the time the snapshot was created. Any changes made to the original database are not reflected in the snapshot. Database snapshots are useful for running reports against historical data and for providing a consistent view of data for certain applications.

2. **Filegroup snapshot**: A filegroup snapshot is a point-in-time, read-only copy of a single filegroup within a database. It is created from an existing database and allows users to query the data as it existed at the time the snapshot was created. Any changes made to the original database are not reflected in the snapshot. Filegroup snapshots are useful for rapidly restoring specific filegroups or pages in the event of a failure.

Database snapshots can be used in a variety of scenarios, including:

1. **Reporting and analytics**: Database snapshots can be used to create reports and run analytics against historical data without impacting the performance of the production database. This is particularly useful in scenarios where the production database is heavily used and cannot afford to experience performance degradation.

2. **Testing and development**: Database snapshots can be used by developers to create a copy of the production database and test new code or changes before deploying to production. This helps to ensure that changes are thoroughly tested and do not cause issues in production.

3. **Backup and recovery**: Filegroup snapshots can be used to rapidly restore specific filegroups or pages in the event of a failure. This can help to minimize downtime and ensure that critical data can be quickly restored.

In order to create a database snapshot in SQL Server, you can use the following T-SQL code:

```
CREATE DATABASE database_name_snapshot ON
(
    NAME = database_name,
    FILENAME = 'snapshot_file_path'
)
AS SNAPSHOT OF database_name;
```

To create a filegroup snapshot, you can use the following T-SQL code:

```
CREATE DATABASE database_name_snapshot ON
(
    NAME = filegroup_name,
    FILENAME = 'snapshot_file_path'
)
AS SNAPSHOT OF database_name;
```

Overall, database snapshots are a powerful feature in SQL Server that can be used to improve performance, enable testing and development, and provide a quick and easy backup and recovery solution.

5.10   How do you monitor and manage SQL Server Integration Services (SSIS) package execution and performance?

SQL Server Integration Services (SSIS) is a powerful tool for data integration and transformation. Like any other tool or system, it is important to monitor and manage its execution and performance. In this answer, I will provide an overview of how to monitor and manage SSIS package execution and performance.

1. Implement logging: Logging is a very important feature of SSIS that allows you to track package execution and troubleshoot issues. There are various logging options available in SSIS, such as Text File, SQL Server, and Event Log. You can choose the appropriate logging option based on your requirements. Enabling logging will provide you with valuable information on package execution, such as start time, end time, execution status, and any errors or warnings encountered during execution.

Here is an example of how to enable logging in SSIS:

```
- Open the SSIS package in Visual Studio
- Go to SSIS Menu -> Logging...
- Add a new log provider and specify the logging details, such as the
      destination and format of the log
- Select the appropriate events to log, such as OnPreExecute, OnPostExecute,
      and OnError
- Save and close the package
```

2. Use performance counters: Performance counters are a great way to monitor SSIS package performance. You can use the SQL Server

Performance Monitor or any other tool that supports performance counters to monitor SSIS package performance. Some of the key performance counters that you can monitor include:

```
- Buffer memory: This counter gives you an idea of the amount of memory used
    by the buffer manager during package execution.
- Rows read and written: These counters give you an idea of the amount of
    data being read from and written to the data source and destination.
- Package execution time: This counter gives you an idea of how long the
    package is taking to execute.
```

3. Analyze package execution with SSIS Catalog reports: The SSIS Catalog provides a number of built-in reports that can help you monitor and manage SSIS package execution. Some of the reports that you can use include:

```
- Execution Performance Report: This report provides a summary of package
    execution, including start time, end time, duration, and status.
- All Executions Report: This report provides a list of all package executions
    , including execution details, status, and start time.
- All Messages Report: This report provides a list of all messages generated
    during package execution, including information on errors and warnings.
```

4. Use checkpoints: Checkpoints are a feature in SSIS that allows you to restart a package from the point of failure instead of starting from the beginning. This can be particularly useful for large packages that take a long time to execute. To use checkpoints, you need to configure the package to use checkpoints and specify a checkpoint file.

Here is an example of how to enable checkpoints in SSIS:

```
- Open the SSIS package in Visual Studio
- Go to SSIS Menu -> Package Configurations...
- Select the Enable checkpoints option
- Specify the location and name of the checkpoint file
- Save and close the package
```

In conclusion, monitoring and managing SSIS package execution and performance is a critical task for any DBA or data professional. By implementing logging, using performance counters, analyzing package execution with SSIS Catalog reports, and using checkpoints, you can effectively monitor and manage your SSIS packages.

5.11   What is the role of SQL Server Master Data Services (MDS) in master data management?

SQL Server Master Data Services (MDS) is a master data management tool that supports creating and managing a centralized repository of business-critical data such as customer, product or financial data. MDS enables users to define, manage, and maintain master data and hierarchies independently of other systems, such as transactional systems.

MDS provides a platform for managing master data and enables organizations to develop a common definition of data, establish data governance policies and processes, and maintain consistent data across an enterprise. Some of the key features of MDS are:

1. **Data Modeling**: MDS enables users to create and maintain a centralized data model that defines the structure of master data. Users can define entities, attributes, and relationships between entities.

2. **Data Management**: MDS provides a centralized repository for storing master data. Users can create, edit, and delete master data using web-based tools or Excel.

3. **Data Governance**: MDS supports data governance by providing tools for managing data quality, establishing data ownership, and enforcing data standards.

4. **Data Integration**: MDS can integrate with other systems, such as ERP systems, CRM systems or data warehouses, to enable the exchange of master data.

5. **Versioning and Validation**: MDS provides versioning capabilities that enable users to manage different versions of master data. MDS also provides validation rules that ensure the consistency and accuracy of master data.

In summary, MDS plays a critical role in master data management by providing a centralized platform for managing master data and enabling users to define, manage, and maintain consistent master data across an organization.

5.12   Can you explain the concept of temporal tables in SQL Server, and what are their benefits?

Temporal tables are a new feature in SQL Server 2016 that allow the storage of historical data in a simple way, without the need for complex queries or custom code. A temporal table is a database table that stores the history of data changes over time. When a row is updated or deleted, a new row is created in the table to store the old values, along with the new values in the original row. This allows for easy auditing and recovery of data from previous points in time, without having to rely on backups or custom code.

To create a temporal table in SQL Server, you need to specify the history table and the period columns. The history table is a separate table that stores the historical data, and the period columns represent the time range during which the data was valid. Here is an example:

```
CREATE TABLE Customers
(
    CustomerID INT PRIMARY KEY,
    Name VARCHAR(50),
    Email VARCHAR(50),
    ValidFrom DATETIME2(0) GENERATED ALWAYS AS ROW START,
    ValidTo DATETIME2(0) GENERATED ALWAYS AS ROW END,
    PERIOD FOR SYSTEM_TIME (ValidFrom, ValidTo)
)
WITH (SYSTEM_VERSIONING = ON (HISTORY_TABLE = dbo.CustomersHistory));
```

In this example, the Customers table has two period columns ('Valid-From' and 'ValidTo') that define the time range during which each row was valid. The 'SYSTEM_VERSIONING' clause specifies that the table is a temporal table, and the 'HISTORY_TABLE' option specifies the name of the history table.

One of the main benefits of temporal tables is their ability to simplify auditing and compliance. By storing historical data in the same table, you can easily track changes to your data over time and meet regulatory requirements. Additionally, temporal tables can make it easier to recover lost data because you can retrieve previous versions of the data by querying the history table.

Another benefit is that temporal tables allow for easy analysis of changes over time. For example, you can easily create reports that show how data has changed over a certain period, or how often certain data has been changed. This can be valuable for trend analysis, troubleshooting, and other purposes.

Overall, temporal tables are a powerful feature that simplify data auditing and analysis, while also reducing the need for custom code and complex queries.

5.13   How do you use SQL Server's Policy-Based Management to enforce and manage database configuration policies?

SQL Server's Policy-Based Management (PBM) is a powerful tool that allows database administrators to enforce and maintain database configuration policies across their SQL Server infrastructure. PBM provides a centralized way to create, evaluate, and enforce policies across one or more SQL Server instances in a consistent and automated manner.

To use PBM to manage database configuration policies, you need to follow these steps:

1. Create a Policy Management Facet:

The first step is to create a Policy Management Facet that will hold the policies. The Policy Management Facet is essentially a container that defines the scope of policies. It can be created and managed through SQL Server Management Studio (SSMS) or via T-SQL. A facet is a collection of properties that is relevant to the item being managed; for example, a database or a server. You can create a policy management facet by either using the SSMS object explorer or using the CREATE FACET statement in T-SQL.

2. Create a Policy:

Once the Policy Management Facet is in place, the next step is to define policies that will be used to manage the configuration settings. A policy is a set of conditions and actions that are used to ensure that a certain aspect of database configuration is managed according to the requirements of your organization. For example, you can design a memory policy to ensure that SQL Server allocates enough memory to meet the requirements of the workload. You can create a policy by using SSMS or T-SQL. To create a policy in SSMS, navigate to the Management folder, right-click on Policy Management, and select New Policy.

3. Define Conditions:

Once the policy is created, you need to define the conditions that must be met to ensure that the policy is enforced. In PBM, conditions are expressed as a combination of logical expressions, operators, and values that define the requirements of the policy. For instance, the memory policy condition can be set to ensure that the minimum memory setting is 4GB.

4. Set Evaluation Mode:

After the conditions are defined, you can set the evaluation mode that will be used to determine if the policies are compliant or not. PBM supports three evaluation modes: On Demand, On Schedule, and On Change. On Demand means that policies are evaluated when you request it. On Schedule means that policies are evaluated according to a schedule. On Change means that policies are evaluated when a specific event occurs, such as a change in server configuration.

5. Define Actions:

Now that you've defined conditions and set evaluation modes, the next step is to define what actions should be taken when a policy is not in compliance. You can define multiple actions for each policy; for example, email a notification to the administrator, do nothing, run a script or remediation.

6. Test and Deploy Policies:

Once policies have been created, their conditions are defined and evaluation modes are set, and actions have been defined, the next step is to test the policies. The best approach is to test policies in a staging environment before applying them to production. When you are ready to deploy policies, you can either push them to target servers manually or automate the deployment through PBM.

In conclusion, Policy-Based Management is a powerful tool that enables database administrators to define, enforce, and manage configuration policies across multiple SQL Server instances. By following the above-mentioned steps, administrators can ensure that their databases are configured according to organization policies and compliance requirements.

5.14   What are the best practices for SQL Server database migration and consolidation?

SQL Server database migration and consolidation are critical tasks for organizations aiming to optimize their data management and reduce costs. In this answer, we will discuss some best practices that can help you successfully complete these tasks.

1. Plan and Prepare: Before beginning any migration or consolidation project, it is essential to have a plan in place. This plan should include the following:

- Identify the scope of the project and define the goals and objectives

- Determine the resources required such as hardware, software, and personnel

- Create a timeline and schedule for the project

- Identify the risks and develop a contingency plan

2. Assess and Analyze: Once the plan is in place, the next step is to assess and analyze the current environment. This involves understanding the current database schema, data types, sizes, and data flow. You also need to identify any dependencies or limitations that may impact the migration or consolidation process.

3. Test and Validate: After completing the assess and analyze phase, it's important to test and validate the migration or consolidation process. This involves creating a test environment that mirrors the production environment and testing the process on a small subset of the data.

4. Back up and Restore: Back up all data before starting the migration or consolidation process. Ensure that backups are stored in a secure location and have been tested to ensure a successful restore.

5. Minimize Downtime: Minimizing downtime during migration or consolidation is critical to minimizing the impact on end-users. You can use techniques such as database mirroring, log shipping, and replication to keep the data synchronized during the migration process.

6. Monitor and Tune: Check the performance of your databases before and after migration. Monitor SQL Server performance using Microsoft's built-in features such as SQL Server Performance Monitor or third-party tools, and use tuning techniques such as index maintenance to optimize database performance.

7. Document and Review: After completing the migration or consolidation process, it's important to document the changes made and review the process to identify areas for improvement.

Example: Here is an example of SQL Server migration using the SQL Server Import Wizard. Assume you have a database named "myDB" on a SQL Server instance and you want to migrate it to a new instance on a different server.

1. First, back up the "myDB" database on the source server using SQL Server Management Studio (SSMS).

2. Launch the Import and Export Data wizard from SSMS on the destination server and select the "SQL Server Native Client" as the data source.

3. Connect to the source server and select the "myDB" database as the source database.

4. Select the destination server and create the destination database by specifying a name, file location, and other relevant settings.

5. Choose the tables or views you want to migrate and configure any necessary mappings or transformations.

6. Review and validate the migration settings and run the migration process.

7. Once the process is complete, verify that the data has been successfully migrated and validate any necessary changes needed due to data and schema differences.

In summary, SQL Server database migration and consolidation are complex processes that require careful planning, preparation, and execution. Following these best practices can help minimize risks, reduce downtime, and ensure a successful outcome.

5.15   How do you optimize the SQL Server Query Optimizer and Cardinality Estimator for better query performance?

The SQL Server Query Optimizer is responsible for generating an optimal execution plan to execute a query based on database schema, query logic, and statistics. The Cardinality Estimator is a component of the Query Optimizer that estimates the number of rows returned by a query. To optimize the Query Optimizer and Cardinality Estimator for better query performance, there are several best practices to follow:

1. Use up-to-date statistics: Accurate and current statistics help the Query Optimizer to generate optimal execution plans. Hence, it is recommended to keep statistics updated by enabling auto-update statistics or manual statistics updates.

2. Consider using the latest compatibility level of your database: Compatibility level determines the Query Optimizer version and behavior. Using the latest compatible level ensures that the database uses the latest Query Optimizer version.

3. Avoid using non-SARGable expressions in WHERE clauses: Non-SARGable expressions such as functions, calculations, and type conversions inhibit the use of an index and result in scan operations that increase query execution time. Therefore, it is recommended to use SARGable expressions in WHERE clauses.

4. Use appropriate index types: Indexes improve query performance by reducing the number of rows accessed during query execution. Clustered indexes are recommended for queries that sort and group data while non-clustered indexes are recommended for queries that filter data.

5. Avoid overusing JOIN and UNION operators: Overusing JOIN and UNION operators require the Query Optimizer to consider multiple execution plans, which results in slower query performance. Hence, it is recommended to use the appropriate JOIN and UNION operators that improve query performance.

6. Avoid using the NOLOCK hint: The NOLOCK hint allows for dirty reads, which can return inconsistent data due to uncommitted changes. It is recommended to use READ_COMMITTED isolation level instead.

7. Optimize queries by understanding query execution plans: Understanding query execution plans helps identify inefficiencies that can be optimized in the query or schema.

8. Partition large tables: Partitioning large tables distribute data across multiple file groups, making data retrieval faster and improving query performance.

9. Use appropriate hardware resources: Proper hardware resources such as CPU, RAM, and I/O resources play a vital role in query performance. Therefore, it is essential to use appropriate hardware resources to optimize the Query Optimizer and Cardinality Estimator.

To summarize, optimizing the SQL Server Query Optimizer and Cardinality Estimator involves using up-to-date statistics, using the latest compatibility level, using SARGable expressions in WHERE clauses, using appropriate index types, avoiding overusing JOIN and UNION operators, avoiding using the NOLOCK hint, optimizing queries, partitioning large tables, and using appropriate hardware resources.

5.16 What are the key considerations for implementing a hybrid SQL Server environment with cloud integration?

Hybrid SQL Server environment refers to an architecture in which databases are distributed between on-premises servers and cloud servers, enabling the integration of cloud services into the SQL Server environment. This can be achieved in several ways, including the use of SQL Server in a virtual machine in a public cloud or with a cloud database service such as Azure SQL Database. In this context, there are several key considerations to keep in mind when implementing a hybrid SQL Server environment with cloud integration:

1. Security: Security is a critical aspect to consider when moving databases to the cloud. Ensuring that data is encrypted both at rest and in transit is crucial for safeguarding sensitive information. Implementing proper access control and authentication mechanisms is also essential in ensuring that only authorized users have access to the data. Depending on the type of cloud services used for the hybrid environment, additional security measures may be necessary.

2. Performance: When integrating cloud services with on-premises databases, network performance becomes a crucial factor. Ensuring that the network bandwidth and latency are optimized for efficient data transfer is essential in minimizing the impact of cloud services on application response times.

3. Data Integration: Data integration between on-premises and cloud databases is another critical consideration. This involves ensuring that data is synchronized between the different instances of the database, ensuring data integrity, and minimizing data inconsistencies. Depending on the specific use case, different approaches can be used, including replication, backup and restore or data movement services.

4. Licensing: Licensing considerations are essential when implementing a hybrid SQL Server environment with cloud integration. Different cloud services have different licensing requirements, and organizations need to ensure that they have the necessary licenses to deploy their databases in the cloud.

5. Monitoring and management: Maintaining proper monitoring and

management of the SQL Server environment is critical for identifying performance issues, security threats, and detecting potential issues before they become critical problems. Utilizing different tools and automating tasks can help in streamlining management and reducing administrative overhead.

In summary, implementing a hybrid SQL Server environment with cloud integration requires significant planning and consideration of many factors, including security, performance, data integration, licensing, and management. By addressing these factors, organizations can move towards a more modern and agile SQL Server environment, take advantage of the scalability and flexibility of cloud services, while maintaining full control over their data.

5.17 How do you monitor and manage SQL Server Analysis Services (SSAS) cube processing and performance?

Monitoring and managing SQL Server Analysis Services (SSAS) cube processing and performance is important in ensuring optimal performance and minimizing downtime. Here are some tips for doing so:

1. Monitor SSAS cube processing: SSAS cube processing can take a significant amount of time and resources, and it's important to monitor the process to ensure it completes successfully and within a reasonable timeframe. You can use SQL Server Management Studio (SSMS) or SQL Server Data Tools (SSDT) to monitor processing status and performance statistics. You can also use DMVs (Dynamic Management Views) and DMFs (Dynamic Management Functions) to monitor processing progress and performance metrics. For example, you can use the "$System.DISCOVER_OBJECT_ACTIVITY" DMV to monitor processing activity, or the "$System.MDSCHEMA_MEASUREGROUP_DIMENSIONS" DMV to get information about dimension usage in a cube.

2. Optimize cube processing: To improve cube processing performance, you can optimize cube and dimension design, optimize queries, and optimize processing settings. For example, you can use incremental processing to avoid processing unnecessary data, use processing

partitions to process parts of the cube concurrently, and use parallel processing to take advantage of multiple CPUs. You can also use aggregation design to optimize query performance, and cache frequently accessed data to reduce processing time.

3. Monitor SSAS cube performance: Once a cube is deployed, it's important to monitor its performance to ensure it's meeting performance targets and to identify performance bottlenecks. You can use SSMS or SSDT to monitor query performance and resource utilization. You can also use DMVs and DMFs to get performance metrics, such as memory usage, processor time, and query execution time. For example, you can use the "$System.MDSCHEMA_MEASURE-GROUP_DIMENSIONS" DMV to analyze query patterns and identify potentially inefficient queries.

4. Optimize SSAS cube performance: To optimize cube performance, you can use techniques such as aggregation design, partitioning, and query optimization. You can also use tools such as Analysis Services Processing Best Practice Analyzer and SQL Server Profiler to identify and diagnose performance issues.

In addition to these tips, it's important to regularly review and optimize SSAS cube design and processing to ensure optimal performance and efficiency.

5.18   What are the best practices for SQL Server backup and recovery planning?

SQL Server backup and recovery planning is crucial to ensure the availability of data in case of any disaster or data loss. Here are some best practices that can be followed for SQL Server backup and recovery planning:

1. Determine the criticality of the data: It is important to determine the criticality of the data based on the business needs. This will help in identifying the backup and recovery strategy that needs to be implemented.

2. Implement a backup strategy: A backup strategy must be im-

plemented based on the criticality of the data. The backup strategy should include the frequency of backups, type of backup (full, differential, or incremental), and the retention period of the backups. It is important to ensure that backups are taken regularly and stored securely.

3. Test the backups: It is important to test the backups periodically to ensure that they can be restored when required. Testing the backups will also help in identifying any issues before they turn into disasters.

4. Implement a recovery strategy: A recovery strategy should be implemented based on the criticality of the data. The recovery strategy should include the time required to restore the data, the recovery point objective (RPO) and the recovery time objective (RTO). The RPO is the maximum tolerable amount of data loss, and the RTO is the maximum tolerable downtime.

5. Implement a disaster recovery plan: A disaster recovery plan should be implemented to ensure that data can be recovered in case of any disaster. The disaster recovery plan should include the steps that need to be taken, the roles and responsibilities of the team members, and the communication plan.

Example of code to take a full backup of a database:

```
BACKUP DATABASE [AdventureWorks2016]
TO DISK = N'C:\Backup\AdventureWorks2016.bak'
WITH NOFORMAT, NOINIT, NAME = N'AdventureWorks2016-Full Database Backup',
SKIP, NOREWIND, NOUNLOAD, STATS = 10
GO
```

Example of code to restore a full backup of a database:

```
USE [master]
RESTORE DATABASE [AdventureWorks2016]
FROM DISK = N'C:\Backup\AdventureWorks2016.bak'
WITH FILE = 1, MOVE N'AdventureWorks2016_Data' TO N'C:\Data\
    AdventureWorks2016.mdf',
MOVE N'AdventureWorks2016_Log' TO N'C:\Log\AdventureWorks2016.ldf',
NOUNLOAD, STATS = 5
GO
```

Overall, SQL Server backup and recovery planning is crucial for the availability of critical data. Following these best practices will help to minimize downtime and ensure the availability of the data in case of any disaster or data loss.

5.19   Can you explain the concept of distributed transactions and the role of the Microsoft Distributed Transaction Coordinator (MSDTC) in SQL Server?

Distributed transactions refer to transactions that involve multiple resources, such as databases, applications, or other data services, that are located on different servers or machines. The purpose of a distributed transaction is to ensure that all resources involved in the transaction are either committed or rolled back as a single unit of work. In a distributed transaction, a coordinator is responsible for managing the transaction, ensuring that all resources are informed about the state of the transaction, and coordinating the commit or rollback process.

The Microsoft Distributed Transaction Coordinator (MSDTC) is a transaction manager that provides distributed transaction management for applications and databases running on Windows servers. MSDTC is also used in SQL Server to coordinate distributed transactions across multiple instances or databases, even if those instances are on different servers.

When an application executes a distributed transaction, MSDTC takes charge of the transaction management process. MSDTC creates a transaction object, which is used to manage the transaction across multiple resources. MSDTC then coordinates the transaction state and ensures that all resources are informed about the state of the transaction. If any of the resources involved in the transaction fail, MSDTC will initiate a rollback of the entire transaction.

In SQL Server, MSDTC plays a key role in managing distributed transactions that involve multiple database instances. MSDTC allows a transaction to be started on one instance and then extended to additional instances as needed. This allows transactions to be completed across multiple instances as a single unit of work.

Here is an example of how MSDTC is used in SQL Server:

```
BEGIN DISTRIBUTED TRANSACTION
```

```
INSERT INTO Server1.Database1.dbo.Table1 (Column1, Column2)
VALUES (Value1, Value2)

INSERT INTO Server2.Database2.dbo.Table2 (Column1, Column2)
VALUES (Value1, Value2)

COMMIT TRANSACTION
```

In this example, a distributed transaction is started using the 'BE-GIN DISTRIBUTED TRANSACTION' statement. Two INSERT statements are executed, one against a table on Server1 and another against a table on Server2. Both of these databases are participating in the distributed transaction. Once complete, the transaction is committed using the 'COMMIT TRANSACTION' statement. MSDTC ensures that all resources involved in the transaction are committed or rolled back as a single unit of work.

5.20   How do you use SQL Server In-Memory OLTP features to improve performance for memory-optimized tables and natively compiled stored procedures?

SQL Server In-Memory OLTP is a feature that allows you to improve the performance of memory-optimized tables and natively compiled stored procedures. This feature enables you to use memory-optimized tables, indexes, and natively compiled stored procedures to achieve higher performance and scalability than traditional disk-based tables and stored procedures.

Memory-optimized Tables:
Memory-optimized tables are designed to be used in-memory, which means they can be accessed much faster than disk-based tables. When you create a memory-optimized table, you specify the schema and indexes that you want to use. Because the table is stored in memory, there is no need to perform disk I/O operations, which can significantly reduce the latency of queries. Memory-optimized tables can also be accessed by natively compiled stored procedures, which can further improve performance.

Here is an example on how to create a memory-optimized table:

```
CREATE TABLE dbo.MyMemoryOptimizedTable
(
    ID INT NOT NULL PRIMARY KEY NONCLUSTERED HASH WITH (BUCKET_COUNT = 1000000)
        ,
    Name VARCHAR(50) NOT NULL,
    Age INT NOT NULL,
    CONSTRAINT PK_MyMemoryOptimizedTable_ID PRIMARY KEY NONCLUSTERED HASH (ID)
        WITH (BUCKET_COUNT = 1000000),
) WITH (MEMORY_OPTIMIZED=ON, DURABILITY=SCHEMA_ONLY)
```

In the example above, we create a memory-optimized table with a hash index on the ID column. We also specify the durability option as schema-only, which means that the table data is only stored in memory and not on disk.

Natively Compiled Stored Procedures:
Natively compiled stored procedures are compiled into machine code that runs directly on the CPU. This eliminates the overhead of interpreting T-SQL statements at runtime, which can significantly improve performance. Natively compiled stored procedures can only access memory-optimized tables and do not allow any disk I/O operations.

Here is an example of how to create a natively compiled stored procedure:

```
CREATE PROCEDURE dbo.MyNativelyCompiledStoredProc
    WITH NATIVE_COMPILATION, SCHEMABINDING, EXECUTE AS OWNER
AS
BEGIN ATOMIC WITH (TRANSACTION ISOLATION LEVEL=SNAPSHOT, LANGUAGE='us_english'
    )

    DECLARE @Name VARCHAR(50) = 'John'

    SELECT *
    FROM dbo.MyMemoryOptimizedTable
    WHERE Name = @Name

END
```

In the example above, we create a natively compiled stored procedure that selects data from the memory-optimized table we created earlier. The stored procedure is compiled into machine code and executed directly on the CPU, which can significantly improve performance.

In conclusion, using In-Memory OLTP features such as memory-optimized tables and natively compiled stored procedures can help improve the performance of SQL Server databases. By carefully designing and implementing memory-optimized tables and stored procedures, you can achieve higher levels of scalability and performance than with traditional disk-based tables and stored procedures.

Chapter 6

Guru

6.1 How do you design and implement a scalable and high-performance SQL Server architecture for large-scale enterprise applications?

Designing and implementing a scalable and high-performance SQL Server architecture for large-scale enterprise applications requires careful planning and consideration of several factors. Here are some steps that can be followed to achieve this:

1. Determine the hardware and software requirements: The first step in designing a scalable and high-performance SQL Server architecture is to determine the hardware and software requirements. This involves understanding the workload, the data storage and processing requirements, and the budget constraints.

2. Choose the right server: The server should be chosen based on the estimated workload and the budget constraints. Consideration should be given to the number of CPUs, memory, disk storage, and network throughput.

3. Configure storage: Storage is critical to performance in a SQL

Server environment. Consider using RAID to improve read and write times, and use dedicated disks for data, transaction log, tempdb and backups.

4. Use a distributed architecture: Large-scale enterprise applications typically have a distributed architecture with multiple servers. Using a distributed architecture can improve performance by reducing the workload on individual servers. SQL Server features such as AlwaysOn Availability Groups, Failover Clustering and distributed partitioned views can be used to achieve this.

5. Optimize indexes: Indexes can improve query performance, but they can also negatively impact performance if they are not optimized. Ensure that only necessary indexes are created, and consider using the Database Engine Tuning Advisor to recommend index strategies.

6. Use stored procedures: Stored procedures can improve performance by reducing network traffic and improving query optimization. Consider encapsulating all data access within stored procedures.

7. Implement caching: Caching can help reduce the load on the database server by storing frequently used data in memory. Consider using tools such as Redis or Memcached to implement caching.

8. Monitor performance: Monitoring is important to ensure that the system is performing optimally. SQL Server provides a range of performance monitoring tools, including SQL Profiler and the Dynamic Management Views.

In summary, designing and implementing a scalable and high-performance SQL Server architecture for large-scale enterprise applications requires careful planning and consideration of several factors. By choosing the right hardware and software, optimizing configuration and performance, and monitoring the system performance, it is possible to achieve a high-performance, scalable architecture that can support large-scale enterprise applications.

6.2   What are the advanced techniques for SQL Server query optimization and performance tuning?

SQL Server query optimization and performance tuning are critical aspects of database management. Whether you are dealing with a small or large-scale application, optimizing query performance can help reduce server load, enhance user experience, and scale your application accordingly. In this answer, we will explore the advanced techniques for SQL Server query optimization and performance tuning.

1. Update Statistics: Indexes help to speed up SQL Server queries, and statistics play a crucial role in the performance of these indexes. SQL Server keeps statistics about data distribution in each column of a table. It is essential to keep these statistics up to date as it influences the query optimizer's decision-making process. Stale statistics can mislead the optimizer into making the wrong choices.

The following SQL commands can help update statistics:

```
-- Update statistics for a table
UPDATE STATISTICS table_name;

-- Update all statistics for all tables in a database
EXEC sp_updatestats;
```

2. Index Optimization: Proper indexing is crucial for high-performance queries. You can boost query performance by creating indexes based on the selection criteria that the queries are using. SQL Server provides different types of indexes: Clustered, Non-Clustered, and Full-Text. The choice of an index is determined by the query type.

For example, a clustered index is suitable for queries that involve range searches or sorting, while a non-clustered index is ideal for queries that seek a specific value from a table.

To optimize indexing, you can use SQL Server's Index Tuning Wizard, as well as SQL Profiler, to identify slow-running queries and implement the necessary indexing.

3. Query Optimization: Query optimization involves reviewing the structure and content of queries to enhance performance. In addition

to creating indexes, several techniques help optimize query performance, including:

- Reducing the number of joins
- Avoiding functions in WHERE clauses
- Minimizing subqueries
- Using efficient data types
- Partitioning tables

4. Stored Procedure Optimization: Stored procedures are essential database objects, and optimizing their performance can enhance the application's overall performance. To optimize stored procedures, you can:

- Use input parameters to filter queries
- Avoid using temporary tables or table variables
- Ensure that indexes are present where necessary
- Use only the necessary columns in SELECT statements.

5. Query Analysis Tools: SQL Server includes several tools that allow you to analyze query performance, including SQL Profiler, Database Engine Tuning Advisor, and Performance Monitor. Using these tools can help you identify issues that impact query performance and take the necessary measures to optimize queries.

In conclusion, SQL Server query optimization and performance tuning are essential aspects of a well-designed database system. By keeping statistics up to date, optimizing indexing, improving query performance, optimizing stored procedures, and utilizing query analysis tools, you can ensure that your application performs optimally, even as the data grows.

6.3 How do you evaluate and choose between different SQL Server high availability and disaster recovery solutions for specific business scenarios?

Choosing the right high availability (HA) and disaster recovery (DR) solution for SQL Server depends on several factors such as the business requirements, budget, infrastructure, RTO and RPO targets, and data growth. In this answer, we will discuss some of the common SQL Server HA/DR solutions and the factors that companies should consider when evaluating and selecting the right solution for their business.

1. Always On Availability Groups
Always On Availability Groups (AG) is a SQL Server feature that provides high availability and disaster recovery capabilities by replicating databases to multiple secondary replicas. AGs support automatic failover and manual failover, depending on the configuration. Companies can use AGs for both local and remote DR scenarios.

When evaluating Always On AG, some of the factors to consider include:

- Compatibility: AGs require Enterprise Edition of SQL Server and Windows Server Failover Clustering (WSFC). Companies should ensure that their infrastructure supports these requirements.

- RPO and RTO: Always On AG allows for synchronous and asynchronous replication, providing different levels of RPO and RTO. Companies should consider their recovery time objectives and recovery point objectives when choosing between synchronous and asynchronous replication.

- Cost: Enterprise Edition of SQL Server is expensive, and the cost of licensing and hardware requirements for AGs can be significant.

- Scalability: Always On AG can handle up to eight secondary replicas for a particular primary replica. Companies with large databases and high data growth should consider whether AG can scale to meet their needs.

2. Failover Cluster Instances
Failover Cluster Instances (FCI) is a SQL Server feature that provides HA by clustering multiple SQL Server instances on different nodes of

a Windows Server Failover Cluster. In the event of a failure, the cluster will automatically failover to a healthy node.

When evaluating FCI, consider the following:

- Compatibility: FCI requires SQL Server Enterprise Edition and Windows Server Failover Clustering. Companies should ensure that their infrastructure supports these requirements.

- Cost: Licensing and hardware requirements can be significant for FCI solutions.

- Complexity: FCI requires more complex infrastructure and maintenance than other HA solutions, including shared storage and cluster nodes.

- Scalability: FCI is limited to two nodes per cluster, so companies that require more nodes may need to consider other solutions.

3. Log Shipping
Log Shipping is a SQL Server feature that replicates transaction logs from a primary database to one or more secondary databases. This solution provides DR capabilities and can be set up asynchronously, meaning that the secondary database is not updated in real-time.

When evaluating Log Shipping, consider the following:

- RPO and RTO: Log Shipping provides a minimum of 15 minutes RPO, and it can take longer to bring the secondary database online in the event of a failure.

- Cost: Log Shipping is included with SQL Server and can be a cost-effective solution.

- Scalability: Log Shipping can handle large databases, but it is not as scalable as Always On AG.

4. Database Mirroring
Database Mirroring is a deprecated SQL Server feature that allows for SQL Server instances to mirror the database from the primary server to a secondary server. Database Mirroring can provide high availability and can be set up to be asynchronous.

When evaluating Database Mirroring, consider the following:

- Compatibility: Database Mirroring is compatible with Standard, Enterprise and Datacenter editions of SQL Server and can only mirror individual databases.

- RPO and RTO: Database Mirroring provides a minimum of 15 minutes RPO.

- Cost: Database Mirroring is included with SQL Server and can be a cost-effective solution.

- Availability: Database Mirroring has been deprecated since SQL Server 2012, and while it is still available in SQL Server 2017, Microsoft recommends moving to Always On Availability Groups for high availability scenarios.

Conclusion:
Choosing the right HA and DR solution for SQL Server is dependent on various factors such as cost, infrastructure, RPO and RTO targets, and data growth. By evaluating the above solutions' compatibility, RPO, RTO, cost, scalability, and availability, companies can make the best choice for their business scenarios.

6.4 Can you discuss the advanced security features in SQL Server, such as Always Encrypted, Data Masking, and Row-Level Security, and their implementation strategies?

SQL Server provides several advanced security features to enable secure data access and protection. In this answer, we will discuss three of these features: Always Encrypted, Data Masking, and Row-Level Security.

Always Encrypted

Always Encrypted is a feature that enables encryption of sensitive data at rest and in transit. It provides end-to-end encryption by ensuring that sensitive data is encrypted both on the client-side and when stored in the database. Even database administrators and others who have access to the database do not have access to the encryption keys that are required to decrypt sensitive data.

To use Always Encrypted, you need to create an encryption key hi-

erarchy that includes a column master key and a column encryption
key. The column master key is stored in a key store, while the column encryption key is used to encrypt and decrypt the data. You
can create a column encryption key using various algorithms, such as
AES and RSA.

Here is an example of how to enable Always Encrypted for a column
in a table:

```
--create column master key
CREATE COLUMN MASTER KEY MyCMK
WITH
    (
        KEY_STORE_PROVIDER_NAME = 'MSSQL_CERTIFICATE_STORE',
        KEY_PATH = 'CurrentUser/My/AEColumnMasterKey',
        ENCRYPTION_TYPE = RSA_OAEP,
        CREATE_NEW = TRUE
    );

--create column encryption key
CREATE COLUMN ENCRYPTION KEY MyCEK
WITH
    (
        COLUMN_MASTER_KEY = MyCMK,
        ALGORITHM = 'RSA_OAEP',
        ENCRYPTED_VALUE = <encrypted_value>
    );

--create a table with an encrypted column
CREATE TABLE Employee
(
    EmpID INT PRIMARY KEY,
    Name NVARCHAR(50),
    Salary NVARCHAR(20) COLLATE Latin1_General_BIN2 ENCRYPTED WITH (
        COLUMN_ENCRYPTION_KEY = MyCEK, ENCRYPTION_TYPE = RANDOMIZED,
        ALGORITHM = 'AEAD_AES_256_CBC_HMAC_SHA_256')
);
```

In the above example, a column master key and a column encryption
key are created. Then we create a table with an encrypted column
using the column encryption key. The 'ENCRYPTION_TYPE' parameter specifies the type of encryption used, and the 'ALGORITHM'
parameter specifies the encryption algorithm.

Data Masking

Data Masking is a security feature that helps protect sensitive data
by obscuring it from non-privileged users. It is used to hide sensitive
data from unauthorized personnel while still allowing privileged users
to access it.

To use Data Masking, you can define a masking rule for a column
that replaces the sensitive data with non-sensitive data. You can

use different types of masking functions, such as random data, or a custom string.

Here is an example of how to use data masking to mask a column in a table:

```
--add a new column with masked data to the existing table
ALTER TABLE Employee
ADD MaskedSalary NVARCHAR(20) MASKED WITH (FUNCTION = 'default()') NULL;
```

In the above example, a new column named 'MaskedSalary' is added to the table. The 'MASKED WITH' parameter specifies the masking function that should be used. In this case, we use the 'default()' function to mask the data .

Row-Level Security

Row-Level Security (RLS) is a feature that restricts access to rows in a table based on user-specific criteria. It enables you to define security policies that are applied to rows in a table, so that users can only view or modify the rows that are associated with them.

To use RLS, you can define a security predicate for a table that identifies which rows should be visible to a specific user based on the user's credentials or attributes. You can also define a security function that performs a more complex calculation to determine which rows should be visible.

Here is an example of how to use row-level security to restrict access to rows in a table:

```
--create a security policy
CREATE SECURITY POLICY EmployeeFilter
ADD FILTER PREDICATE EmployeeFilterPredicate(EmployeeID)
ON Employee WITH (STATE = ON);

--create a security function that does the filtering
CREATE FUNCTION EmployeeFilterPredicate(@empid int)
RETURNS TABLE
WITH SCHEMABINDING
AS
    RETURN
        SELECT 1 AS fn_securitypredicate_result
        WHERE @empid = CAST(SESSION_CONTEXT(N'empid') AS int);
```

In the above example, we create a security policy that restricts access to rows in the 'Employee' table. We then create a security function that does the filtering based on the employee id defined in the session parameters. The 'SESSION_CONTEXT' function is used to retrieve the employee id from the session parameters.

To summarize, Always Encrypted, Data Masking, and Row-Level Security are advanced security features in SQL Server that enable secure data access and protection. Each of these features has its own implementation strategies and can be used in combination to provide an even more secure environment.

6.5   What are the best practices for managing and maintaining a multi-tenant SQL Server environment?

A multi-tenant SQL Server environment is one where multiple customers (i.e., tenants) share physical database resources. It requires careful management and maintenance to ensure the reliable, secure, and efficient operation of the database. Here are some best practices for managing and maintaining a multi-tenant SQL Server environment:

1. Database Design: Use a database design that accommodates multiple tenants. A common approach would be to have a single database with a separate schema for each tenant, and each tenant schema contains tables, stored procedures, and other database objects.

2. Security: Ensure that each tenant is provided with their own unique login credentials and that they can only access their own data. This can be achieved by implementing Row-Level Security (RLS) or by using separate schemas for each tenant.

3. Resource Allocation: Consider implementing resource allocation plans to ensure that each tenant is provided a fair share of database resources like CPU, Memory, Disk IO, etc. Resource Allocation is usually performed using Resource Governor feature in SQL Server.

4. Backup and Recovery: Backup and recovery mechanisms must be implemented properly. A schedule should be in place for regular backups to ensure tenants' data safety. A strategy should be defined for disaster recovery, including options for Restoring data to Point-in-time in case of data loss as well as restoring the database to different

hardware in case of a whole data center failure.

5. Monitoring: Monitoring must be done carefully, using various SQL Server monitoring tools (SQL Server Profiler, DMVs, SQL Server Extended Events, etc.). Monitor usage statistics to identify any tenants who might be using excessive resources or could be considered as a security threat. Also, keep track of resource utilization and growth trends to identify when the database requires scaling up.

6. SLA Management: Employ Service Level Agreements (SLAs) with tenants that clearly describe the services offered, support levels provided, performance expectations, and compliance requirements. Establish thresholds for performance metrics like response time, CPU and Disk usage, etc. So that you can trigger alerts whenever SLA thresholds are violated.

7. Automation: Use automation wherever possible to handle routine tasks like backups, monitoring, and resource allocation. By automating repetitive tasks, you can reduce the burden on your database team, avoid human errors, and increase reliability.

In summary, managing a multi-tenant SQL Server environment requires careful consideration for security, database design, resource allocation, maintenance, and monitoring. By following these best practices, you can ensure that your database effectively meets the needs of each tenant while maintaining optimal performance, reliability, and security.

6.6   How can you leverage machine learning and artificial intelligence capabilities in SQL Server, such as using R or Python with SQL Server Machine Learning Services?

SQL Server Machine Learning Services (formerly known as SQL Server R Services) is a feature that allows users to run R and Python scripts in SQL Server. This integration enables data scientists and developers to leverage the powerful machine learning and artificial intelligence capabilities of R and Python within their SQL Server environment, which can bring significant benefits in terms of efficiency, scalability, and security.

To use Machine Learning Services in SQL Server, you need to have SQL Server 2016 (or later) Enterprise Edition or Standard Edition with Service Pack 1. You also need to install either R or Python language runtime, as well as the respective libraries for data manipulation and analysis, visualization, and machine learning.

Here are the main steps to follow to use R or Python with SQL Server Machine Learning Services:

1. Install R or Python and their respective libraries on your SQL Server instance. You can do this by using the SQL Server installer, which includes a component called "Machine Learning Server (Standalone)", or by downloading and installing the runtime and libraries separately.

2. Enable and configure Machine Learning Services in SQL Server by running a script in the SQL Server Management Studio (SSMS). This script sets up the required system databases, endpoints, and permissions for Machine Learning Services to work properly.

3. Write R or Python code for data processing, analysis, and machine learning, and embed it in a stored procedure or a script file. You can use any R or Python library that is compatible with Machine Learning Services, including popular ones such as Pandas, NumPy, Scikit-Learn, TensorFlow, Keras, and ggplot2.

4. Execute the R or Python code from SQL Server by calling the stored procedure or running the script file. The code will run in a secure and isolated process within the SQL Server instance, and will be able to access and manipulate data from the SQL Server tables or views.

Here is an example of a simple R script that calculates the mean and standard deviation of a column in a SQL Server table:

```
# Load the required R packages
library(RevoScaleR)
library(sqlrutils)

# Connect to the SQL Server database
sqlConn <- RxSqlServerConnect(server = "myServer", database = "myDatabase")
```

```
# Define the SQL query to retrieve the data
sqlQuery <- "SELECT myColumn FROM myTable"

# Retrieve the data into an R data frame
myData <- RxExec(sqlQuery, connectionString = sqlConn)

# Calculate the mean and standard deviation of the data
myMean <- mean(myData$myColumn)
mySd <- sd(myData$myColumn)

# Print the results
print(paste("Mean:", myMean, "SD:", mySd))

# Disconnect from the SQL Server database
RxSqlServerDisconnect(sqlConn)
```

This script uses the RevoScaleR and sqlrutils packages to connect to
a SQL Server database, retrieve a column of data from a table using
a SQL query, and perform some basic statistics on the data using R
functions. The result is printed in the console output.

In summary, by using R or Python with SQL Server Machine Learning Services, you can bring the power of machine learning and artificial intelligence to your SQL Server environment, and integrate data
processing, analysis, and visualization seamlessly with your database
operations. This integration can lead to faster insights, better accuracy, and more efficient workflows.

6.7 What are the strategies for optimiz-
ing and managing large-scale data warehousing and business intelligence solutions with SQL Server?

Optimizing and managing large-scale data warehousing and business
intelligence solutions with SQL Server requires a comprehensive approach that encompasses several strategies. In this answer, we will
discuss some of the key strategies for optimizing and managing large-
scale data warehousing and business intelligence solutions.

1. Proper data modeling: Proper data modeling is the foundation
of any data warehousing solution. In a large-scale data warehousing solution, it is even more critical to ensure that the data model
is optimized for performance. The data modeling should take into
account the queries that are going to be run against the database,

the expected data volumes and distribution, and the hardware that
will be used to host the database.

2. Partitioning: Partitioning is the process of dividing large tables
and indexes into smaller, more manageable pieces. Partitioning can
help to improve query performance by reducing the amount of data
that needs to be scanned. SQL Server supports partitioning of tables
and indexes based on a partitioning function. Partitioning can also
improve data load and maintenance operations by providing more
granular control over the data.

3. Indexing: Proper indexing is critical to achieving optimal query
performance in a large-scale data warehousing solution. Since OLAP
queries typically involve aggregations and filtering, indexes should be
designed accordingly. Consider using columnstore indexes, filtered
indexes, and indexed views to improve query performance.

4. Compression: Data compression can be an effective way to reduce the storage requirements of large-scale data warehousing solutions. SQL Server supports both row-level and page-level compression. Row-level compression can help to reduce the size of large tables, while page-level compression can improve query performance by
reducing the amount of data that needs to be read from disk.

5. Query optimization: Query optimization is critical to achieving optimal performance in a large-scale data warehousing solution. Consider using query hints, such as MAXDOP, to improve query performance. Also, consider using parallelism to speed up queries by
processing data in parallel.

6. Monitoring and tuning: Monitoring and tuning is an ongoing
process that involves monitoring database performance metrics and
making adjustments as needed. SQL Server provides several tools for
monitoring and tuning database performance, including SQL Server
Management Studio, SQL Server Profiler, and Performance Monitor.

7. Hardware optimization: Proper hardware configuration is critical
to achieving optimal performance in a large-scale data warehousing
solution. Consider using a storage area network (SAN) to improve
disk performance, and make sure that the database server has enough
memory to accommodate the working set of data and queries.

In summary, optimizing and managing large-scale data warehousing and business intelligence solutions with SQL Server requires a comprehensive approach that encompasses several strategies, including proper data modeling, partitioning, indexing, compression, query optimization, monitoring and tuning, and hardware optimization. By applying these strategies, organizations can achieve optimal performance in their data warehousing and business intelligence solutions.

6.8 How do you design and implement a robust SQL Server monitoring and alerting system for proactive issue resolution and performance management?

Designing and implementing a robust SQL Server monitoring and alerting system is critical to ensure that the SQL Server database is performing at optimal levels and to identify and resolve issues before they become critical. A well-designed monitoring system will also provide insight into resource utilization and help identify current and future capacity requirements.

Follow the steps given below to design and implement a robust monitoring and alerting system:

Step 1: Define monitoring requirements

Define the monitoring requirements based on the business needs of the organization. Define the metrics that need to be monitored and choose tools that can collect and monitor the required metrics.

Step 2: Choose a Monitoring Tool

Choose a monitoring tool that can collect, store and analyze the metric data. SQL Server Management Studio (SSMS) can be used to collect basic metrics. Advanced enterprise level monitoring can be implemented using third party tools like SQL Monitor or SQL Sentry.

Step 3: Define Baselines and Thresholds

Define baseline values for the monitored metrics, including acceptable ranges and thresholds. This will help determine when the metric values have strayed beyond normal performance standards, and give DBAs warning of impending problems.

Step 4: Implement automation for alerts and notifications

Automate alerts and notifications using SMS, e-mail, or other notification programs. This will help the DBA staff to respond proactively instead of reacting when a performance issue arises.

Step 5: Monitor system performance

Monitor the system performance metrics such as CPU usage, memory usage, I/O bandwidth and storage utilization. These metrics provide insights into the overall health of the system and help identify potential bottlenecks that could be hindering performance.

Step 6: Monitor SQL Server instances

Monitor SQL Server instances and collect performance data to identify performance issues that could be impacting the database. Some of the critical metrics that need to be monitored include: wait times, SQL server wait stats and query execution plans.

Step 7: Review and tune the alert thresholds

Review and tune the alert thresholds regularly to ensure that alerts are being generated at the right time – not so early that they swamp the monitoring team with false positives, or so late that they can lead to performance degradation.

Step 8: Establish formal monitoring procedures

Establish formal monitoring procedures that document the monitoring process, the metrics that are monitored, the thresholds that trigger alerts, the response protocol when an alert is issued, and how the monitoring system is maintained.

In summary, designing and implementing a robust SQL Server monitoring and alerting system is critical to ensuring optimal system performance, identifying potential issues before they become significant problems, and supporting proactive, efficient database management.

6.9   What are the key considerations and best practices for migrating complex SQL Server environments to the cloud, such as Azure SQL Database or Amazon RDS?

Migrating complex SQL Server environments to the cloud can be a daunting task, as there are several key considerations and best practices that must be taken into account to ensure a successful migration. Here are some important considerations and best practices for migrating complex SQL Server environments to Azure SQL Database or Amazon RDS:

1. Evaluate the scale and scope of the migration: It is critical to evaluate the scale and scope of the migration, including the number of databases, their sizes, and the frequency of data updates. This will help you determine the appropriate migration approach and identify any potential issues beforehand.

2. Choose the right migration approach: There are several migration approaches available for migrating SQL Server databases to the cloud, including lift-and-shift, re-platforming, and modernization. It is important to choose the right approach based on the specific needs of your environment.

3. Adapt your applications to the cloud: Once your SQL Server databases are migrated to the cloud, it is important to adapt your applications to work in the new environment. This may include modifying connection strings, reviewing object names, and updating stored procedures, among other tasks.

4. Review and optimize performance: Cloud database platforms have different performance characteristics than on-premises SQL Server installations, so it is important to review and optimize the performance of your migrated databases to ensure they perform well in the new environment.

5. Implement security best practices: Migrating databases to the cloud requires implementing security best practices to ensure they are secure and comply with applicable regulations. This includes setting

appropriate access controls, encrypting data, and regular monitoring and auditing.

6. Implement disaster recovery strategies: Migrating databases to the cloud requires implementing disaster recovery strategies to ensure your data is protected in the event of an outage or other disaster. This may include setting up database backups, replication, and high availability options.

7. Consider costs and pricing models: Migrating databases to the cloud can be cost-effective, but it is important to consider the costs and pricing models of the cloud provider. This includes understanding the pricing structure for storage, data transfer, and compute resources.

In summary, migrating complex SQL Server environments to the cloud requires careful planning and execution. By following these key considerations and best practices, you can ensure a successful migration and realize the benefits of cloud-based database platforms such as Azure SQL Database or Amazon RDS.

6.10   How do you manage the performance and scalability of SQL Server Reporting Services (SSRS) and Power BI in large-scale reporting environments?

Managing the performance and scalability of SQL Server Reporting Services (SSRS) and Power BI in large-scale reporting environments involves implementing a variety of techniques and best practices to optimize database and report performance, accommodate user growth, and ensure overall system stability. Below are some essential considerations to keep in mind:

1. Hardware and network capacity planning: Proper hardware and network capacity planning is critical to support the performance and scalability of both SSRS and Power BI solutions. This includes assessing the number of report users, data size, memory, network bandwidth, and disk space required. You should ensure that both the

server hardware and network architecture are properly sized and provisioned for the expected workload.

2. Query optimization: Optimizing queries is another critical aspect of managing SSRS and Power BI performance. Performance issues often arise from poorly optimized queries that consume too many resources. Ensure that you understand the data model and implement appropriate indexing, partitioning, and query tuning strategies. This may involve restructuring the data by utilizing normalized or denormalized tables, creating indexed views, or using columnstore indexes.

3. Report design optimization: Proper report design is essential for optimal performance and scalability. Heavy visualizations or complex report layouts can be demanding on server resources, leading to slower report rendering times. Ensure that you use best practices in report design such as minimizing groups, eliminating blank spaces, using table or matrix formats instead of lists, and grouping filters where possible.

4. Caching and data retrieval performance: SSRS and Power BI caching features can improve report performance by storing query and report data in memory, minimizing the amount of roundtrips to the database. You should consider enabling cache settings for frequently accessed data and reports. Additionally, ensure that the data retrieval from the database is efficient with appropriate use of filters on large datasets.

5. Load balancing and scale-out: As user demand for reports increases, it may be necessary to scale out the SSRS or Power BI environment to accommodate additional users and increase capacity. Using load balancing and clustering technologies can distribute requests across multiple servers, reducing the workload on individual servers, and allowing for horizontal scaling of the deployment.

6. Monitoring and tuning: Monitoring the SSRS and Power BI environment is critical for maintaining optimal performance and scalability. You should monitor data retrieval performance, report render times, server utilization, and network performance regularly. Tuning of the server configuration and queries can be done based on the monitoring results.

In summary, managing the performance and scalability of SSRS and

Power BI in large-scale reporting environments requires proper planning, optimization of queries, report design, caching, load balancing, monitoring, and tuning of the solution. By following best practices in these areas, efficient reporting, high availability, and scalability can be achieved.

6.11 What are the advanced techniques for managing SQL Server Integration Services (SSIS) package development, deployment, and performance optimization?

SQL Server Integration Services (SSIS) is a platform for building data integration and transformation solutions that can connect to various sources and destinations. Here are some advanced techniques for managing SSIS package development, deployment, and performance optimization:

1. Package Configurations: SSIS provides a feature called package configurations that allows the package settings to be stored and retrieved from an external configuration file. This makes it easy to change the package settings without changing the package itself.

2. Logging: SSIS provides a flexible logging framework that allows information about package execution to be captured and stored for later analysis. This helps to diagnose issues and identify performance bottlenecks.

3. Checkpoints: Checkpoints allow packages to restart from a known point after a failure, instead of restarting from the beginning. This can save time and resources, especially for packages with long execution times.

4. Deployments: SSIS packages can be deployed using various methods such as deployment utility, scripts or SSDT. Deployment should be done systematically and the packages should be tested after deployment.

5. Connection Managers: Connection Managers are used to define connections to data sources, and can be configured to optimize performance. For example, the OLE DB connection manager can be configured to use connection pooling, which can reduce the time required to establish a connection to a database.

6. Buffering: SSIS packages use buffers to move data between components. Buffer size can be tuned to optimize performance depending on the data source, speed of the network and other factors.

7. Parallelism: The Data Flow task in SSIS runs components in parallel by default. Parallel execution can scale a package to take advantage of the available resources and improve overall performance.

8. Optimizing Data Flows: There are a number of techniques to optimize data flows in SSIS such as sorting, aggregating, and using lookup caches. These techniques can be used to improve the performance of data transformation tasks.

9. Design Patterns: SSIS design patterns are reusable solutions to common integration scenarios. They are a set of guidelines and best practices that can be used to simplify package development, and improve performance and maintainability.

10. Performance Monitoring: To optimize SSIS packages, it is important to monitor performance metrics such as CPU usage, memory usage, and disk I/O. This can be done using Windows Performance Monitor or by using third-party monitoring tools.

In summary, managing SSIS package development, deployment, and performance optimization involves a variety of advanced techniques such as package configurations, logging, checkpoints, deployments, connection managers, buffering, parallelism, optimizing data flows, design patterns, and performance monitoring. By leveraging these techniques, you can develop and deploy robust and high-performance SSIS solutions.

6.12   Can you discuss the strategies for implementing and managing cross-platform and heterogeneous database environments with SQL Server?

In enterprise environments, it is common to have multiple database systems operating across different platforms. SQL Server, as a relational database management system, must be designed to operate in heterogeneous database environments. Below are some strategies for implementing and managing cross-platform and heterogeneous database environments with SQL Server:

1. Data Integration: Data integration tools such as SQL Server Integration Services (SSIS), can be used to integrate data from various data sources, including data from heterogeneous platforms. SSIS includes data sources, transformations, and destinations that can help to access, transform, and load data from various platforms using a single solution.

2. Data Replication: SQL Server also provides data replication tools, which can be used to replicate data across platforms. Replication can be used to replicate data from one SQL server to another, as well as to replicate data from non-SQL server databases to SQL servers. SQL Server supports different types of replication topologies including snapshot replication, transactional replication, and merge replication.

3. SQL Server Linked Servers: Linked Servers allow SQL servers to access data from heterogeneous database systems. Linked servers allow Transact-SQL (T-SQL) statements to be executed against the remote data sources.

4. Query Optimization: When querying data from heterogeneous platforms, query optimization becomes essential. SQL Server query optimizer analyzes each query and generates an execution plan. This execution plan can be optimized using the SQL Server Query Analyzer or SQL Server Management Studio.

5. Centralized Management: In a heterogeneous database environment, managing all the data sources and ensuring data availability becomes critical. SQL Server provides a centralized management

platform through SQL Server Management Studio.

6. Monitoring and Troubleshooting: It is important to monitor and troubleshoot any issues that arise in a heterogeneous database environment. SQL Server's built-in performance monitoring and troubleshooting tools such as Dynamic Management Views (DMVs) and SQL Server Profiler can help identify and troubleshoot issues in a heterogeneous environment.

In conclusion, implementing and managing cross-platform and heterogeneous database environments is a challenging task. With the above strategies, SQL Server can be used to provide a unified platform to manage data from multiple platforms. Data integration, replication, Linked Servers, query optimization, centralized management, and monitoring and troubleshooting are some of the key strategies SQL Server provides to support heterogeneous database environments.

6.13   How do you plan and implement a comprehensive SQL Server auditing and compliance strategy?

Planning and implementing a comprehensive SQL Server auditing and compliance strategy involves several steps, including:

1. Identify regulatory requirements: The first step is to identify the regulatory requirements that apply to your organization, such as HIPAA, PCI DSS, or SOX. Each regulation may have specific requirements for auditing and compliance, so it is important to understand them.

2. Define scope: Determine the scope of your auditing and compliance strategy. Which databases, tables or columns will be audited? Which users or groups will be monitored? Which events will be audited? Etc.

3. Determine the auditing level: SQL server has three different auditing levels: server, database and object level. Each level captures information differently and has its own configuration. Define the level that suits your organization's needs, and configure it accordingly.

4. Set up auditing: Configure auditing for SQL Server, including creating audit specifications, audit objects, and audit actions. SQL Server provides a variety of audit actions, including login/logout events, object access, and administrative actions. A complete list of available audit actions can be found in the SQL documentation.

5. Monitor and analyze auditing data: Once auditing is configured, it is important to monitor and analyze the data generated by the audit. This will enable the organization to identify potential security breaches, policy violations, or other issues that require action. SQL Server provides several tools for analyzing audit data, including the SQL Server Audit Log Viewer, SQL Audit Log Reports or any other third-party tool.

6. Develop response procedures: The organization should have procedures for responding to audit findings. This includes notifying appropriate parties, conducting investigations, and taking remedial actions, if necessary.

7. Review and update the strategy periodically: As regulations change and technology advances, it is important to review and update the auditing and compliance strategy periodically to ensure that it remains effective.

To help understand the steps needed to plan and configure a comprehensive SQL Server auditing and compliance strategy, here is an example on how you can compose an audit specification within a database:

```
CREATE SERVER AUDIT [Audit_Name]
  TO FILE (
    FILEPATH = 'C:Audits'
    ,MAXSIZE = 50 MB
  )
  WITH (
    QUEUE_DELAY = 1000
    ,ON_FAILURE = CONTINUE
);
CREATE DATABASE AUDIT SPECIFICATION [Audit_Spec_Name]
    FOR SERVER AUDIT [Audit_Name]
    ADD (SELECT, INSERT, UPDATE, DELETE, EXECUTE ON OBJECT::[dbo].[Table_Name
        ])
    WITH (STATE = ON);
```

This script creates a server audit and a database audit specification based on the requirements and scope of the organization. The audit specification specifies which actions should be audited on which objects, and the server audit provides where the audit data should be collected.

6.14 What are the advanced techniques for managing and optimizing SQL Server Analysis Services (SSAS) tabular and multidimensional models?

There are several advanced techniques for managing and optimizing SQL Server Analysis Services (SSAS) tabular and multidimensional models. In this answer, some of the important techniques are discussed.

1. Partitioning: Partitioning is a technique that can significantly improve query performance and reduce processing time. Partitioning divides a table into smaller, more manageable pieces called partitions. Each partition can be processed and queried independently, which enables the database engine to process queries in parallel. Partitioning is particularly useful for large tables or tables that store historical data.

2. Aggregations: Aggregations are pre-calculated summaries of data that can be used to speed up queries. In SSAS, aggregations can be created at different levels of granularity, allowing users to query the data quickly without the need to calculate aggregates on the fly. In addition, aggregations can be stored in memory, further improving query performance.

3. Measures and Hierarchies: Measures are the numeric data that are used for analysis in SSAS. Hierarchies are the logical grouping of data in the cube. Optimizing measures and hierarchies can significantly improve query response times. Creating hierarchies can speed up queries by creating rollup calculations on the fly. Measures can be optimized by using different aggregation functions such as sum, count, average, and distinct count.

4. Query Optimization: Query optimization can improve query performance by selecting the most efficient query execution plan. For

example, using indexes, avoiding predicates that cannot be indexed, and optimizing joins can significantly improve query performance. Query optimization can also be achieved by caching frequently used queries, using aggregations and aggregating tables, and using row-level security to restrict access to data.

5. Data Compression: Data compression can reduce the size of the data stored in SSAS, which can improve query performance and reduce memory usage. In SSAS, data compression can be achieved through a technique called column-based compression. Column-based compression reduces the size of data by storing repeated values only once.

6. Processing Modes: There are three processing modes in SSAS: Full, Incremental, and Process Add. Full mode processes the entire database, while Incremental mode processes only the changes since the last processing. Process Add mode processes only the new data added to the database. By using the appropriate processing mode, processing time can be reduced, and query performance can be improved.

In summary, by using techniques such as partitioning, aggregations, measures and hierarchies optimization, query optimization, data compression, and processing modes, SSAS models can be managed and optimized to deliver the best performance.

6.15 How do you design and implement a data archiving and data retention strategy for large-scale SQL Server environments?

Designing and implementing a data archiving and retention strategy for large-scale SQL Server environments involves several steps. These steps can be summarized as follows:

1. Identify the data that needs to be archived or retained: The first step is to identify the data that needs to be archived or retained. This can include historical data, unused tables, and unused columns.

2. Determine the retention and archival requirements: The next step is to determine the retention and archival requirements. This includes identifying how long the data needs to be retained, and how frequently the data needs to be accessed.

3. Create an archival and retention plan: Based on the retention and archival requirements, a plan needs to be created. This includes deciding on the frequency of archiving, the archival location, and the archival process itself.

4. Test the archival and retention plan: Once the plan is created, it needs to be tested. This involves testing the frequency of archival, the archival process, and the accessibility of the archived data.

5. Adjust the plan as needed: Based on the testing results, adjustments may be needed to the plan. This includes adjusting the frequency of archiving or the archival location.

6. Monitor and maintain the archival and retention plan: Once the plan is implemented, it needs to be monitored and maintained. This includes testing the accessibility of the archived data, ensuring the archived data is secure, and performing regular backups of the archived data.

There are several tools and features available in SQL Server that can help with implementing a data archiving and retention strategy.

1. Partitioning: SQL Server partitioning can be used to split large tables into smaller, more manageable pieces. This can make it easier to archive and retain data.

2. Compression: Compressing data can reduce storage requirements and improve overall performance. SQL Server includes several compression options that can be used to compress both data and backups.

3. Backup and restore: SQL Server includes several backup and restore options that can be used to create and restore backups of data. These backups can be used as part of an archival and retention strategy.

4. Archival and retention tools: Several third-party tools are available that can help with implementing a data archiving and retention strategy. These tools can automate the archival process and make it

easier to access archived data.

In addition to these tools and features, it is important to consider security when designing and implementing a data archiving and retention strategy. This includes ensuring that archived data is stored securely, and that access to archived data is limited to authorized users.

Overall, designing and implementing a data archiving and retention strategy for large-scale SQL Server environments requires careful planning, testing, and maintenance. By following best practices and leveraging available tools and features, it is possible to create a robust and effective archival and retention plan.

6.16   What are the key considerations and best practices for implementing and managing real-time data processing and analytics solutions with SQL Server?

Real-time data processing and analytics involve processing and analyzing data as soon as it is generated. SQL Server provides several tools and features that can help in implementing and managing real-time data processing and analytics solutions. The key considerations and best practices for implementing and managing real-time data processing and analytics solutions with SQL Server are as follows:

1. Data Ingestion: Data ingestion is the process of collecting and importing data into a data processing system. SQL Server provides several tools for data ingestion, including SQL Server Integration Services (SSIS), SQL Server Data Factory, and SQL Server Change Data Capture. SSIS is a powerful tool for extracting, transforming, and loading data from various sources. SQL Server Data Factory allows you to create data pipelines to move data between cloud and on-premises data sources. SQL Server Change Data Capture is a feature that captures all changes made to the SQL Server database and makes them available for downstream processing.

2. Data Storage: Real-time data processing and analytics solutions

require a data storage system that is scalable, performant, and reliable. SQL Server provides several options for data storage, including SQL Server databases, SQL Server Analysis Services (SSAS), and SQL Server in-memory technologies such as In-Memory OLTP and Columnstore indexes. SQL Server databases provide a relational database management system that can store structured and semi-structured data. SSAS provides a multi-dimensional view of data and allows for advanced analytics such as data mining and predictive modeling. In-Memory OLTP and Columnstore indexes provide high performance and scalability for real-time data processing and analytics.

3. Data Processing and Analytics: Real-time data processing and analytics require tools and technologies that can analyze data as soon as it is generated. SQL Server provides several tools for real-time data processing and analytics, including SQL Server Analysis Services, SQL Server Reporting Services, and SQL Server PolyBase. SQL Server Analysis Services provides an OLAP cube that can be used for advanced analytics such as data mining and predictive modeling. SQL Server Reporting Services provides a tool for creating and delivering interactive reports. SQL Server PolyBase allows you to analyze data from various external data sources such as Hadoop and Spark.

4. Real-time data monitoring: Real-time data processing and analytics solutions require real-time monitoring to ensure that the system is running smoothly and to identify any issues that arise. SQL Server provides several tools for real-time data monitoring, including SQL Server Performance Monitor and SQL Server Management Studio. SQL Server Performance Monitor provides real-time performance monitoring of SQL Server instances and allows you to view and analyze performance data. SQL Server Management Studio provides a comprehensive view of your SQL Server database and allows you to manage and monitor your databases in real-time.

In conclusion, implementing and managing real-time data processing and analytics solutions with SQL Server requires careful consideration of data ingestion, data storage, data processing and analytics, and real-time data monitoring. SQL Server provides several tools and features that can help in implementing and managing real-time data processing and analytics solutions.

6.17 How do you use advanced features of SQL Server, such as PolyBase and Stretch Database, to integrate and manage big data and distributed data sources?

SQL Server provides advanced features to integrate and manage big data and distributed data sources. Two prominent features are Poly-Base and Stretch Database.

PolyBase allows us to access and query data from external data sources such as Azure SQL Data Warehouse, Hadoop, and Oracle. We can use T-SQL to query data from these sources as if they were part of our SQL Server database. PolyBase enables SQL Server to act as a federated engine, where it can query data stored outside of SQL Server without needing to move the data into SQL Server.

To use PolyBase, we will need to configure the PolyBase services and create the required database objects such as external data sources, external tables, and definitions. Here is an example of querying data from Hadoop using PolyBase:

```
CREATE EXTERNAL DATA SOURCE Hadoop
WITH (LOCATION = 'hdfs://myhadoopcluster:9000');

CREATE EXTERNAL TABLE HadoopTable (
    [col1] INT,
    [col2] NVARCHAR(50),
    [col3] FLOAT
) WITH (
    LOCATION = '/path/to/hadoop/folder',
    DATA_SOURCE = Hadoop
);

SELECT col1, col2, col3
FROM HadoopTable
WHERE col1 > 10;
```

Stretch Database is another feature that allows us to stretch our on-premises data to Azure, improving the performance of our queries that involve large amounts of historical data. When we stretch our data to Azure, SQL Server maintains a link between the local and remote data using a SQL Server database as a logical bridge.

Stretch Database allows us to store historical data in the cloud while

keeping more frequently used data on premises, improving the performance of the local queries while keeping the historical data available.
We can use Stretch Database on selected tables to offload them to
Azure based on a certain condition, such as data that is older than a
certain date. We can also pause or resume data migration to optimize
our workloads.

To use Stretch Database, we need to configure it in SQL Server and
identify the tables that are suitable for stretching. Here is an example
of enabling Stretch Database for a table:

```
ALTER TABLE SalesData
ENABLE REMOTE_DATA_ARCHIVE
WITH (MIGRATION_STATE = ON);
```

In conclusion, PolyBase and Stretch Database are advanced features
in SQL Server that can be used to integrate and manage big data
and distributed data sources. Both features require configuring SQL
Server and creating required database objects to function correctly.

6.18   Can you discuss the latest trends and advancements in SQL Server technology and how they impact database management and development?

SQL Server is constantly evolving, and there have been some significant advances in recent years. Here are a few key trends and
advancements to be aware of:

1. Cloud-based deployments: Cloud computing has become increasingly popular in recent years, and SQL Server is no exception. Microsoft Azure, the company's cloud platform, offers a range of SQL
Server-based options, from fully managed database services to virtual
machines. This move to the cloud has implications for database management, as it introduces new ways of securing, scaling, and accessing
databases.

2. Big Data: As organizations generate and collect more data, they
often require more powerful database tools to manage and analyze it.

SQL Server 2019 introduced Big Data Clusters, which enable users to combine SQL Server with Apache Spark and Hadoop Distributed File System (HDFS). By allowing users to work with both structured and unstructured data in a single environment, Big Data Clusters provide new options for data management and analysis.

3. Artificial intelligence (AI): AI is increasingly being used to help manage and analyze databases. SQL Server 2019 introduced features like Machine Learning Services and the ability to run Python scripts natively. These capabilities can be used to automate routine tasks, identify patterns in data, and perform predictive analytics.

4. Security: SQL Server has always placed a strong emphasis on security, but recent advancements have further enhanced the platform's capabilities. Features like Always Encrypted, Dynamic Data Masking, and Row-Level Security make it easier for administrators to protect sensitive data and ensure compliance with regulations like GDPR and HIPAA.

Overall, these trends and advancements in SQL Server technology are having a significant impact on database management and development. The move to cloud-based deployments and the introduction of new tools for managing and analyzing Big Data are two key areas to watch. At the same time, the growing use of AI and continued emphasis on security will continue to shape the way we use SQL Server in the years to come.

6.19   What are the best practices for managing a globally distributed SQL Server environment with data replication and synchronization across multiple regions?

Managing a globally distributed SQL Server environment can be complex, particularly when dealing with data replication and synchronization across multiple regions. However, there are several best practices that organizations can follow to ensure that their distributed SQL Server environment is efficient, effective, and secure.

1. Use a robust data replication and synchronization solution:

One of the most critical factors in running a distributed SQL Server environment is ensuring that data is replicated and synchronized across all regions in a timely and accurate manner. There are several well-established data replication and synchronization solutions available, such as SQL Server Always On Availability Groups or Merge Replication. Ensure the replication and synchronization solution is not putting any undue pressure on the individual database servers and is capable of handling the workload and any requests.

2. Use a distributed architecture:

Using a distributed architecture can help ensure that the load is evenly distributed across all the database servers. In this manner, requests do not purely bottleneck in one server while leaving the others far behind. Collocate data with its performance dependencies and minimize latency.

3. Monitor database performance:

Regular monitoring of the database servers in each region is critical to identifying and addressing performance issues. Multiple factors can contribute to poor database performance, including high CPU utilization, high memory usage, slow disk access, or a large number of connections to the server. Introduce comprehensive monitoring solutions that enable the team to continually monitor distributed system performance and detect bottlenecks and issues in real-time.

4. Implement Disaster Recovery solutions:

In case of any event or atypical issues, Disaster Recovery solutions should be implemented to reduce the risk of downtime and protect data. These could be, for instance, Backup and Restore, Log Shipping, or Replication.

5. Ensure Data Security:

Ensuring data security is essential in any database management system. In a globally distributed SQL Server environment, additional measures such as enhancing encryption or implementing access control measures, should be in place to ensure data confidentiality and integrity.

6. Automate Monitoring and Maintenance tasks:

Leaving no loose ends or tasks unchecked, automating tasks, will ensure everything is being monitored, such as index fragmentation or tracking server performance. Automation frees up valuable resources, reduces errors, increases system reliability, and ultimately contributes to an improved customer experience.

7. Maintain Database Synergy:

Keeping databases in sync could be achieved through implementing latest data transfer techniques available in all servers, which could include Transactional Replication, Merge Replication or Snapshot Replication.

In conclusion, Managing a globally distributed SQL Server system requires a team effort, taking an integrated approach with best practices on all fronts, such as optimizing the database, hardware, and software. This continually ensures that the system is running smoothly, maintaining a robust architecture, and providing users with the best possible experiential value.

6.20   How do you plan and execute a successful SQL Server version upgrade or migration while minimizing downtime and ensuring data integrity?

Planning and executing a SQL Server version upgrade or migration can be a complex process, but there are several steps that can help minimize downtime and ensure data integrity:

1. Pre-upgrade evaluation: Before upgrading or migrating to a newer version of SQL Server, it is important to evaluate the existing database environment and identify any potential issues or compatibility concerns. This can be done using tools like the Microsoft Upgrade Advisor, which can highlight potential problems such as deprecated features, unsupported configurations, and database compatibility issues. It is also important to ensure that all necessary prerequisites are met

and that sufficient hardware resources are available to support the new version.

2. Back up the database: Prior to carrying out any upgrade or migration, it is critical to perform a full backup of the database. This ensures that a restore point exists in case something goes wrong and allows for a quick recovery in case of any data loss or corruption during the upgrade process.

3. Test the upgrade process: Before upgrading or migrating in a production environment, it is important to test the process in a non-production environment, such as a staging or testing environment. This can help identify any issues or bottlenecks that may occur during the upgrade process and allows for any necessary adjustments to be made before the production upgrade.

4. Schedule downtime: While it is possible to perform an upgrade or migration with minimal downtime using techniques like database mirroring or log shipping, it is usually necessary to schedule some amount of downtime in order to complete the process. This can be done during a maintenance window or during a period when system usage is typically low.

5. Perform the upgrade: Once all necessary preparations have been made, the upgrade can be carried out. This typically involves running the SQL Server Setup program and selecting the appropriate upgrade or migration options. During the upgrade process, SQL Server will automatically upgrade the database schema, data files, and other system components to the newer version.

6. Validate the upgrade: Once the upgrade is complete, it is important to validate that the new version of SQL Server is functioning correctly and that all necessary configuration settings and options have been retained. This can be accomplished by running tests or performance benchmarks in the new environment, reviewing system logs and error messages, and performing spot checks of data integrity.

By following these steps, it is possible to carry out a successful SQL Server version upgrade or migration while minimizing downtime and ensuring data integrity. Of course, the specific steps and procedures may vary depending on the specific upgrade scenario and requirements. It is also important to have a backup and recovery plan in place and to be prepared for any potential issues or problems that may arise during the upgrade process.

www.ingramcontent.com/pod-product-compliance
Lightning Source LLC
LaVergne TN
LVHW051338050326
832903LV00031B/3610